THE EMPEROR'S NEW KILT

THE EMPEROR'S NEW KILT

THE TWO SECRET HISTORIES OF SCOTLAND

JAN-ANDREW HENDERSON

MAINSTREAM
PUBLISHING

EDINBURGH AND LONDON

First published in Great Britain in 2000 by
MAINSTREAM PUBLISHING COMPANY (EDINBURGH) LTD
7 Albany Street
Edinburgh EH1 3UG

ISBN 1 84018 378 0

Cover photograph © John McAviney

A catalogue record for this book is available from the British Library

Typeset in Allise and Van Dijck
Printed and bound in Great Britain by Cox & Wyman Ltd

There is only one thing wrong with Scotsmen, there are too few of them.
WINSTON CHURCHILL (1874–1965), ADDRESSING THE HOUSE OF COMMONS

The typical Scot has bad teeth, a good chance of cancer, a liver under severe stress and a heart attack pending. He smokes like a chimney, drinks like a fish and regularly makes an exhibition of himself. He is forever trying to cover up the pathological cracks in his character.
JOURNALIST ALAN BOLD (1943–)

Here's tae us; wha's like us? Damn few an' they're a' deid.
SCOTTISH TOAST

ACKNOWLEDGEMENTS

I'd like to acknowledge the people who have given love, encouragement, research time and cigarettes. Thanks to Mum and Dad, Emily, Claire (T.), Nichola, Siobhan, all the guides at St Giles' Cathedral, Jan I., Kate and Katherine.

CONTENTS

INTRODUCTION

The Emperor stood in front of the mirror admiring the clothes he couldn't see.
  'Am I not magnificent?' he asked his courtiers.
Not wishing to be thought stupid or disloyal, the courtiers replied,
  'Oh how they suit you!' and 'A perfect fit!'
  'Now to show my people', said the Emperor, 'I shall have a procession.
  HANS CHRISTIAN ANDERSEN, *THE EMPEROR'S NEW CLOTHES*

Did you know that most tartans date from August 1822? Or that the kilt was invented by an Englishman? Or that Robert the Bruce inadvertently started the Ku Klux Klan?

On the other hand, did you know that a Scottish expedition explored America a century before Columbus? Or that the city of Dundee had electric lighting 70 years before Thomas Edison invented the light bulb?

The history of Scotland has always been fascinating – no other country has managed to combine fact and legend so superbly that nobody can distinguish one from the other. Indeed, many of the most famous Scottish images have the most dubious origins. The world-famous Highland Games are a perfect example. Events like tossing the caber may not have the panache of Olympic events (then again, the Highland Games don't have the hop, skip and jump) but they do have a valid historical connection. In the years after the Jacobite Rebellions, when highlanders were prohibited from owning weapons, these tests of strength were how would-be combatants kept themselves toned up.

But the star of the Highland Games, apart from the beer tent, is the Scottish dancer. There are monks in Tibet who have postcards of Scottish dancers – pre-pubescent girls in mini-kilts and velvet jackets prancing up and down on top of blunt crossed swords. Yet, when you stop to think about what these dancers are actually doing, this most popular of tourist attractions is a parody of everything it is supposed to stand for. The highlanders were warriors who stamped and crashed their feet in time to the wail of the bagpipes, working themselves into a fighting frenzy and their enemies into a state of terror. When they danced on swords, they were the bloody swords of fallen enemies.

Scottish dancing, on the other hand, is as effeminate a pastime as is humanly possible – with costumes to match and more steps than the Eiffel Tower. The whole enterprise couldn't be further removed from what it is supposed to represent.

It is sometimes very difficult to work out what is genuinely Scottish and what isn't – and the Scots themselves don't help. Often they have bought into their own mythology without finding out or caring about its authenticity.

Highland cows, for instance, are as popular a subject for postcards as the Highland dancer, so everyone assumes that they are ancient Scottish beasts. Highland cattle have indeed been roaming the northern hills for centuries – but they were small and dark. The long-haired, bright orange 'coos' that are famous in Scotland today are the result of cross-breeding in Europe in the eighteenth century.

The beautiful landscapes of the north are a similar case. Many of Scotland's vast forests of pine, so appealing to the tourist, were planted in the last century. The country's indigenous species was the silver birch, now almost eradicated. Upper New York State looks more like ancient Scotland than modern Scotland does.

But taking offence at these particular aspects of Scotland is fruitless. Highland cattle were black – now they are orange. The Highlands were covered in birch, now they're covered in pine. Either way, you don't get hairy orange cows anywhere else and a hillside covered in regular rows of pine can still take the breath away. They are as Scottish now as the kilt or the tartan.

The problem is, just how Scottish exactly are kilts and tartans?

That's what I have tried to address in this book – and the results might come as a bit of a a shock.

The Emperor's New Kilt, however, does not knock down Scottish myths for the sake of it, although it's great fun. No. In stripping away the fable you find out what's really underneath. That often means finding something unpleasant – and the case of Scotland is no exception. But to a far greater extent, what is underneath is something exceptional – and that's a very pleasant find indeed.

It's odd. The Scots are a nation who will tell everyone within earshot, and at great length, how good they are at fighting. Then they'll tell you how they invented everything in the world. And then they'll tell you how good they are at fighting again. There's so much bluster there that the Scots have forgotten that, yes, they really did invent a quite astonishing number of things and, yes, they were quite good at fighting. But there was so much more to the Scottish nation than that.

It's a question of balance. Many Scots heroes don't turn out to be as admirable as they first appear, and some of the nation's most famous images are based on pure Scotch mist. On the other hand, the Scots influenced the world in ways they hardly comprehend and, consequently, have never been given credit for. Admittedly, influencing the world is not necessarily a good thing – after all, Hitler did it – but this book isn't designed to make moral judgements on Scottish handiwork, just to point it out.

Scotland has two secret histories. The bad side has been covered up by an avalanche of tartan dolls and shortbread – and some of its most impressive achievements have also been buried under the same pile.

This book is an attempt to quieten some of the bluster. To scrub off some of the whitewash and see what comes up. There's no denying that fable is a powerful force and will always beat truth in a fair fight – and truth itself is hard to pin down. A few of the things I've written about (but only a few) can't be proved beyond a shadow of a doubt.

Yet I've got close enough to cast a large shadow across the 'accepted' truth – and that's valuable enough. I've tried to nudge away a legendary past and celebrate the history that slipped by, unnoticed, in this fake tartan pageant.

Scotland has two secret histories. One records all the things that

Scots are famous for but shouldn't be – the other chronicles the things they are not famous for, but should be.

Of course, all history is subjective.

But no other subject has quite such a history.

McARTHUR

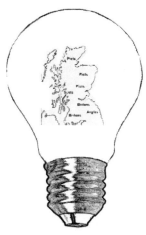

Small and mean though this place is, great and special honour will be
conferred upon it, not only by the kings of the Scots and their
people, but also by the rulers of barbarous and foreign nations.

ADOMNAN, *LIFE OF COLUMBA*

It has long been accepted that the legendary King Arthur is based on
a real historical character. Legends very often are. The problem arises
when anyone tries to work out exactly who he was. Though historians
are a fairly peaceable bunch, the Arthur debate has led to historical
fisticuffs which the Knights of the Round Table would have been hard
pushed to quell.

Over the years, however, most people have come to accept that the
original Arthur was either English or, more probably, Welsh, and that he
lived around the sixth century AD. Though no historical character has
been found that really fits the bill, most medieval writings place the
legendary king in south western Britain and, over the centuries, the
notion that this mythical Dudley-Do-Right was Welsh has worked its
way into the national consciousness.

Yet there is no real evidence to support the notion that Arthur lived in Wales, though several sources are regarded as proof of Arthur being a character from Welsh antiquity. For instance, a Welsh monk named Nennius wrote a short history in the ninth century, edited in the tenth century by Mark the Anchorite. One section of this history mentions a military leader called Arthur, who won 12 battles against the Saxons. Nennius also wrote, however, that Arthur managed to slay 940 Saxons on his own at the battle of Bodon – making one wonder why he needed any knights at all. Another indication of Nennius's spin-doctoring is the fact that two of the battles took place 100 years apart.

Of course, the creation of a legend almost always requires embellishment, but one aspect of Nennius's Arthur is conspicuous by its absence. The monk never actually claims that Arthur is a Welshman (or a Briton, as they were called then). He merely says that Arthur fought *with* the kings of Briton against the Saxons. It has been assumed that because Nennius was Welsh, Arthur must be too, but Nennius gives no description of Arthur's lineage.

If Arthur was fighting the Saxons, of course, it is natural to assume that he would have been fighting in southern England, the Saxon stronghold at that time. It must be noted, however, that Nennius and his contemporaries also called the people of Bernicia 'Saxons'. Yet Bernicia was situated in north-east England and stretched into south-east Scotland. It was the historian Bede who pointed out that Bernicians were not actually Saxons, but Angles.

The Arthur described by Nennius, in that case, might have just as easily been fighting in southern Scotland, not England or Wales, as is popularly thought. Nennius, in fact, might have been describing a sixth century war fought between the Britons of southern Scotland and their enemies, the Picts and Angles. In those battles a real historical character emerges, who has not been considered before. The Britons were aided by one Arturius, son of the Scots King Aiden. Arturius was not a king of the Scots himself, he was only a prince. But Nennius specifically states that Arthur is a leader – not necessarily a king.

The Annals of Wales are also traditionally used as proof for a southern Arthur – the chronicles mention both an Arthur and a Medraut (sounding acceptably close to the name of his legendary enemy Mordred) dying in battle. However, parts of the Welsh Annals were copied from earlier Irish Annals and feature Irish and Scots characters. And, once again, the Welsh Annals don't say who Arthur actually is.

The ancient poem, the *Gododdin*, also mentions the legendary Arthur. But although the Gododdin tribe inhabited Wales, they originally came from the Lothian region of southern Scotland – the area where the Scots prince Arturius died in battle against the Picts. This gives credence to the notion that Arturius died aiding Welsh Britons in southern Scotland in battles against the Angles and the Picts and that he may even have been the leader of a Scottish–Briton coalition.

It was in the twelfth century that the legend of King Arthur really took off, thanks mainly to the writings of Geoffrey of Monmouth. Monmouth knew how to spin an exciting yarn and he wasn't about to let anything as mundane as the truth get in his way. He was the first to claim that Arthur was a king, and a king of Britain at that. He also placed Arthur's kingdom firmly in the south – Cornwall to be exact – though he had no historical evidence whatsoever to back this up.

It made no difference. Later chroniclers simply accepted Monmouth's version as the truth and Tintagel Castle in Cornwall still has a thriving tourist industry based on Arthur to this day.

The lack of a southern 'Arthur' to match the legends has led many researchers to ignore the name altogether. Instead they assert that King 'Arthur' must have been based on someone with an entirely different name.

Yet, as we have seen, there is a historical character who matches the legends and really does have the same name. He just happens to be Scots.

Arturius, in fact, is the earliest recorded example of the name Arthur in Britain. He makes his first appearance in the seventh century chronicle *Life of Columba*, written on the Scots island of Iona by an Irish monk called Adomnan (c.625–704). Arturius was the son of King Aiden of Dalriada (d.606), a territory covering the area now known as Argyll in southern Scotland. Aiden's coronation was possibly the first Christian coronation in Britain and the warrior king was as confrontational as he was pious. He led the Scots in a series of battles against the Picts and Angles before being soundly defeated in Northumbria in 603. It is not hard to see that his son would follow the same path. The *Life of Columba* tells of Arturius's battles against the Picts around the Lothian area near Edinburgh and, although prone to the same wild exaggerations, this chronicle is a century older than the Nennius manuscript.

The *Life of Columba* marks an episode in the life of Arturius's father:

> The saint questioned king Aiden about a successor to the
> kingdom. When he answered that he did not know which of his
> three sons should reign, Arthur, or Echoid Find, or Domingart,

> the saint then spoke in this manner: 'None of these three will
> be king; for they will fall in battles, slain by enemies'.

The story may be a tad implausible, but it does echo the prophetic quality of Arthurian legend – with Columba, famed for performing miracles, fitting the role of Merlin. The Annals of Tighernac, based on eleventh century sources, by an Irish monk called Tighernac, also mention Arturius's death – and here he is called Artuir.

There are other inescapable similarities between Arturius and the legendary King Arthur, similarities not matched by any other historical character. For a start, the name is virtually identical. Arturius, like Arthur, was the son of a powerful king. Like Arthur, he was a Christian warrior at a time when much of the country was still pagan. Arturius was an ally of King Urien – a genuine historical figure who is also mentioned, in legend, as an ally of King Arthur.

Arturius died in battle against the Picts. In the legend, King Arthur died fighting Mordred, whose mother was married to Lot – King of the Picts. Most persuasively, the eighth century document *Martyrology of Oengus the Culdee* states that Arturius had a sister or half-sister called Morgan. In legend, of course, Morgan was the sister of King Arthur. The coincidences are too startling to ignore.

So why has Arturius, the historical figure who most closely resembles the Arthurian legend, been ignored? There are understandable reasons. If Arthur and his father were part of a Welsh military coalition, it isn't surprising that he would feature in Welsh legend. And the twelfth century stories by Geoffrey of Monmouth, placing Arthur in Cornwall, were immensely influential to later writers.

One might wonder why Monmouth and his contemporary medieval chroniclers did not make the connection with Arturius – but it is possible that they did, and just ignored it. By the twelfth century, the English considered Scotland to be an aggressive and chaotic inferior – their culture corrupted by years of Norman and Saxon troublemakers who had migrated from the south.

The stronger nation always gets to rewrite history, and the legendary hero-king drifted further south as the centuries passed. As the fable grew, Arthur became a square-chinned, justice-seeking paragon of virtue in squeaky-clean armour. Scotland could not possibly have produced such a magnificent leader and certainly wasn't worthy of laying claim to one – it was an affront to southern standards. Instead, his deeds were ascribed to some English or Welsh leader who never actually existed. Arthur and the Knights of the Round Table now bear more resemblance to some Aryan superman fantasy than they do to real human beings – especially not a bunch of primitive, hairy Scots.

This was not the last time that a Scottish hero ended up as an English legend.

As we shall see . . .

SHAKESPEARE HATH MURDERED TRUTH

Life's but a walking shadow, a poor player
That struts and frets his hour upon the stage,
And then is heard no more; it is a tale
Told by an idiot, full of sound and fury,
Signifying nothing.

WILLIAM SHAKESPEARE, *MACBETH*

The first Scottish celebrity to be misrepresented by popular fiction – though certainly not the last – was the legendary villain MacBeth (c.1005–57). MacBeth is probably the most famous of Scotland's kings and, thanks to Mr William Shakespeare, is popularly known as a backstabbing psychopath with the ultimate in nagging wives.

There are, of course, difficulties in establishing the truth of events that happened so long ago, but there is no doubt that Shakespeare was using more than his fair share of poetic licence. In his play he happily included MacDuff as MacBeth's nemesis, even though no such historical character existed. The same is true of Banquo and the witches.

There isn't much point in blaming the Bard. He didn't write the 'Scottish Play' until six centuries after the Scot in question was dead and drew much of his inspiration from Holinshed's *Chronicle*, published only 50 years earlier. Holinshed's account of the rise and fall of MacBeth is a lusty one and it is easy to see why Shakespeare thought that it was worth retelling. But William Shakespeare had political as well as artistic reasons for recounting the tale of MacBeth the way he did – and those politics would not have allowed the truth to come out anyway.

Which is a shame. Because the real story of MacBeth is just as bloody and filled with intrigue as the invented one and had a huge impact on the future of Scotland. It's just completely different from the tale that most people are familiar with.

Before examining MacBeth's role in Scottish history, it's necessary to give a bit of cultural and political background to the events surrounding his reign. MacBeth (full name MacBethad mac Findlaech) came to power in 1040, at the end of Scotland's dark ages. At that time, the country he ruled was known as Alba. The inhabitants were of Celtic origin and their society operated through the ancient clan system. To the north, power was held by the Norsemen under Thorfinn of Orkney, while Northumbria, in the south, was occupied by the Anglo-Saxons. And both posed a threat to the Kingdom of Alba.

In England kingship was hereditary, with the crown passing from father to son. In Alba, however, the High Kings were elected. The new ruler was always from a highborn family, but this system meant the throne was not necessarily guaranteed to fall to the next-of-kin. The would-be monarch had to be considered worthy of office to secure the throne unhindered.

This immediately casts doubt on later interpretations of MacBeth's motives, especially those of later English historians, unfamiliar with northern methods of succession. Though MacBeth did indeed kill Duncan, then High King, this did not guarantee him the throne. MacBeth had a valid hereditary claim to the throne of Alba, but the fact that he was elected High King in Duncan's place is a pointer to the fact that the inhabitants considered him a worthy replacement. MacBeth's easy passage to the throne indicates that he had done something to earn Alba's respect, or Duncan had done something to lose it.

Lady MacBeth has been given the unenviable reputation of a

harridan wife from hell. Shakespeare gave the impression that her strength of will and the influence she exerted over her husband were unnatural qualities. Once again, this stems from an English perception of women in history. The Scottish legal system of the time, and for countless years before that, treated women very differently than its southern counterparts. The ancient Celtic tribes had a matriarchal society – marriage did not hamper the rights of women and they could take elected office on an equal footing with the men. If Lady MacBeth was a strong character who exerted influence over men, this was not necessarily a unique thing. There is absolutely no evidence that she had any real character flaws, never mind being a baby-bashing monster.

If MacBeth really did kill Duncan to become High King of Alba, he didn't murder him in his sleep, he killed him in battle. In those ultra-violent times MacBeth's actions were normal – it was commonplace to succeed to the throne by bumping off whoever happened to be occupying it. A quick look at the events leading up to his coronation is ample proof of that.

When MacBeth was born, Malcolm II (c.954–1018), head of the Athol clan, was High King of Alba. He had been elected after killing the previous High King, Kenneth III – as was the trend. Malcolm's daughter married MacBeth's father, Findlaech MacRuaridh, a Mormaer (or minor king) of the clan Moray. The Moray and Athol families were political rivals, but the fact that MacBeth was the High King's grandson may have afforded him some sort of protection in the coming conflicts.

MacBeth's father was not so lucky . . . he was murdered by his own nephews, Malcolm and Gillecomgain. Malcolm was elected as Mormaer and died nine years later. Gillecomgain was elected in his place and, perhaps to improve his claim to High Kingship, married Gruach – daughter of the murdered Kenneth III.

It didn't work. Malcolm II, now an old man, wanted to keep his clan in power and decided to eliminate as many hostile claimants for kingship as he could. As a powerful Moray, Gillecomgain was an obvious candidate to go, and Malcolm II showed no hesitation in shuffling him off the mortal coil.

MacBeth was elected Mormaer in Gillecomgain's place and he too promptly married Gruach. This was a nice political move – Gruach was directly descended from a High King – but MacBeth also adopted Gillecomgain's son Lulach, a fairly decent thing to do considering that Lulach's father had murdered his own. Though records are scarce, there seems to have been no antagonism between Lulach and his stepfather and the Lady MacBeth certainly didn't show any inclination to bash his brains out against a tree.

Malcolm II died at Glamis in 1018 and his grandson Duncan, also of the clan Athol, became High King in his place.

Duncan has gone down in history as a good and decent king. In fact, there is evidence that he was the opposite. In *The Orygynale Cronykil of Scotland*, Andrew Wyntoun describes the new High King as a 'vicious tyrant' – though, admittedly, this description was written several centuries later.

Duncan was ambitious, if nothing else. He launched simultaneous campaigns against Thorfinn of Orkney in the north and Northumbria in the south. Unfortunately, the campaigns were a complete disaster and Duncan showed a streak of callousness by sending repeated waves of Scots cavalry against the massive defensive walls of Durham. Suffering heavy losses in the south, Duncan reassembled his army and assaulted Thorfinn once more. As a military commander, Duncan just didn't cut it and in 1040, he was soundly defeated, dying in the battle.

Magnus Scotus, in his *Chronican Universal*, states that MacBeth was Duncan's 'general' – if MacBeth did kill Duncan, this would imply treachery on MacBeth's part. Yet it seems unlikely that MacBeth would be Duncan's underling, given the feud between the Athol and Moray clans. MacBeth was not a general or a 'thane', as Shakespeare described him – he was a Mormaer, a king in his own right.

There is no evidence that MacBeth did kill Duncan – it is just as likely that the High King was slain by Thorfinn and his men. There isn't even a good reason to believe that MacBeth was fighting on Duncan's side – it's equally possible that MacBeth was fighting for

Thorfinn. Certainly, once he became High King, he remained on good terms with the Norse king.

So what of MacBeth's reign? Was it the tyrannical rule he is famous for?

Apparently not. Chronicles describe him as a liberal king who ruled productively and generously and Andrew Wyntoun tells us that MacBeth 'did many pleasant acts in the beginning of his reign'. Pleasant is not a word usually associated with MacBeth.

MacBeth ruled successfully for 17 years which, considering the violent times, was quite a feat. In 1050 he went on a pilgrimage to Rome for a year, where he 'scattered alms like seed corn', then returned to find his kingdom still intact – not a sign of an unpopular ruler. MacBeth even exiled Duncan's son, Malcolm, instead of killing him.

And this would prove to be his undoing.

Malcolm Canmore (c.1031–93) had gone to England, at that time ruled by Edward the Confessor. There, he picked up a few English notions, including the idea that Kingship was hereditary and not an elected office. Malcolm decided that, as the son of Duncan, he was the rightful heir to the throne of Alba. Edward the Confessor took the opportunity to gain a grateful ally, and backed him up.

With the English support, Malcolm raised an army and invaded Scotland. In 1057, at Lumphanan, he finally triumphed and killed MacBeth. The dead monarch's stepson, Lulach, tried to fight on but he too was killed, and Malcolm was crowned King of Scotland.

It was the end of the centuries-old tradition of elected kings. From that point on, the rulers of Scotland were declared royal at birth.

Shakespeare was at pains to portray MacBeth as the last ruler of a savage and unsuccessful era, one which would change for the better once he was dead. In fact, after his death, Malcolm and his wife, Margaret, brought an end to centuries of successful Celtic traditions.

Malcolm's reign effectively began the forced Anglicisation of Scotland. He invited hordes of southern nobles to Scotland and he introduced feudalism in direct opposition to the ancient clan system, condemning a huge section of the population to little more than slavery. The Marmaers and chieftains had been fathers to their people. Now the Scots were ruled by Anglo-Norman lords who cared little for their welfare. Margaret, Malcolm's queen, was just as detrimental, doing her utmost to Romanise the Celtic church, which had always striven to maintain its own identity. Malcolm then betrayed his own allies and invaded England, beginning years of hostility between the two nations. If anyone resembles Shakespeare's portrayal of MacBeth and Lady MacBeth, it is Malcolm and Margaret.

Once again, the winner rewrites history – Malcolm's heirs in this case. Malcolm became Scotland's 'Warrior King' and MacBeth the nasty, usurping villain. Gruach is condemned to go down in history as an insane tyrant and Margaret became a saint.

So what were Shakespeare's motives? Certainly he spotted a good yarn in Holinshed's *Chronicle*, but there was more to it than that. After the long reign of Elizabeth I, under which he had prospered, the Bard found himself ruled by her successor – James Stuart – formerly King of Scotland. Though he turned out to be a shrewd man and an able king, James was still an unknown quantity.

Shakespeare set about writing a uniquely Scottish play. He manipulated the story of MacBeth and brought in MacDuff, Banquo and the witches to illustrate certain points. Shakespeare played on James's fervent belief in the evils of witchcraft by stressing their influence on MacBeth's treasonous actions.

Banquo, in the play, represents the Stuart dynasty. Banquo is a man of great honour and decency and his heirs inherit the throne of Scotland through their lineage, not by election or violence. It was a plotline calculated to appeal to the first man to inherit the throne of Britain.

In Shakespeare's play, MacDuff kills MacBeth as an act of revenge, pushing Malcolm – whose dynasty was replaced by the Stuarts – into a minor role. It was yet another way of gaining the approval of the new ruler of his country. Shakespeare certainly knew how to grovel.

There is no denying, however, the power of Shakespeare's play. Despite being historical nonsense, it is one of the masterpieces of English literature.

Up against such talent, the real MacBeth never stood a chance.

THE ACID REIGNS

If kings were just a harmless thing like thee,
A form on paper, not in real life,
Then would this suffering world be free
From many a bloody scene of strife.
WILLIAM WILSON (SCOTS WEAVER),
LINES ON LOOKING AT THE PICTURE OF A KING

I f 'following the lost cause' were a sporting event, the Scots would be
world champions. This unfortunate ability may be put down to
obstinacy, national pride, a sense of faith in the natural order of
things or a dozen other misguided factors. Whatever the reason, the
Scots have always had a tendency to stick by their leaders, no matter
how foolish those leaders were or how disrespectfully they treated their
own subjects.

There have been a few notable exceptions but, in general, Scottish
leaders have benefited from blinkered loyalty on the part of their
common subjects. This fidelity has, in part, helped to give the
impression that Scots royalty were a dedicated and able bunch. In fact,

many Scots leaders showed a shocking tendency to disregard the best interests of their nation.

Scotland began as a fragmented nation ruled by a host of minor and major kings of whom little is known. The same is true of the first real line of Scots monarchs, the House of Alpin, though they ruled from 841 to 1034 AD. Their reign is mainly distinguished by their unerring ability to die violently – and usually at the hand of their successor.

When the House of Canmore inherited the throne, however, the chill winds of change began to blow. The north of the country remained unaffected as always, with the clan chiefs still very much in charge. But southern Scotland was about to change forever, to the horror of its inhabitants.

The reign of the Canmores is sometimes referred to as Scotland's 'Golden Age'. It was certainly golden for the Canmores. Scotland certainly found itself a much-strengthened nation under their rule, but its population had to pay a high price for that potency.

Malcolm Canmore began a policy of inviting southern nobles into Scotland whilst leading attacks south against the very race he wanted to emulate – the interesting strategy of trying to beat 'em and join 'em. To increase his own strength, Malcolm encouraged a huge influx of disaffected Saxon, then Norman, nobles into Scotland and rewarded them with land that belonged to his own people.

These Anglo-Norman barons introduced the feudal system into Lowland Scotland. This was an arrangement whereby the king now owned all the land and parcelled out tracts to nobles in return for their allegiance. Naturally, Malcolm found this imported system very much to his liking. The majority of the population, however, lived and worked on the land – and now had to pay their new, foreign overlords for the privilege of doing so.

In Scotland, the population lived in tribes and the clan system worked more like a large extended family, albeit a violent one, than a political hierarchy. Now there were a small number of masters and a huge underclass of serfs. Scotland, and the position of its Canmore leaders, had been strengthened at the expense of the people.

Malcolm's queen, Margaret, was equally uncaring about the Scots. A Saxon brought up in Hungary, she set about dismantling the fabric of the society that had adopted her. She changed the language of the court from Gaelic to English. She began to disassemble the Celtic church and replace it with Roman Catholicism, a catalyst for war and hatred for hundreds of years to come. That the Scots might have liked their ancient language and religion just fine was of no consequence to Margaret. She lavished riches on her new church – paid for by taxing the overworked natives.

Ironically enough, she was made a saint.

With each Canmore king, feudalisation and Normanisation escalated in Scotland. Duncan II (c.1060–94) was simply an English vassal. Edgar 'The Peaceable' (1097–1107) spent years at the English court and ruled using southern backing. He earned his wimpy nickname from his tendency to give away Scots land to the Normans. His brother Alexander 'The Fierce' (1107–24), on the other hand, was named for the savagery he used in quashing his own subjects. Taking an active interest in matters ecclesiastical, he proceeded to stamp out any traditional Celtic customs which St Margaret had missed. The dichotomy of his reign, like so many other Scots kings, was summed up by the chronicler John of Fordun (c.1320–c.1387):

> A lettered and godly man, very humble and amiable towards
> the clerics and regulars, but terrible beyond measure to the
> rest of his subjects.

It paid more, however, to be a friend of the church than of the people. Churchmen wrote the history books.

Alexander was succeeded by David I (1084–1153), who had spent most of his life at the English court and had an English wife. Today, he enjoys a reputation as a good monarch, but he increased feudalisation in Scotland until it became an Anglo-Norman playground. He also carried on the age-old tradition of biting the hand that feeds. During an invasion of England, while the Scots peasants died valiantly for their king, the imported nobles decided the tide of the battle had turned and changed sides halfway through the fight.

Eventually David's own subjects had enough, rebelling against him twice. His son, Malcolm IV (1141–1214), fared no better, having to quell three separate revolts as he pushed feudalism further north of the Forth and Clyde. His successor, William the Lion (1143–1214), extended a network of sheriffs and justices through the south to keep the peace, but gave these positions of power to Anglo-French officials rather than to Scots. He too pushed north with the hated policy of feudalism, suppressing revolts as he did so. His son Alexander II (c.1198–1249) crushed several northern rebellions and discouraged further unrest with a series of spectacular tortures – including having a baby girl's brains bashed out and using wild horses to tear insurrectionists apart.

Alexander III (1241–86) was the last of the Canmores. By this time the Normanisation of southern Scotland was complete and the peasants had surrendered to the feudal system. One English Chronicler wrote of the Canmore reign:

> Recent kings of Scotland profess themselves to be rather Frenchmen, both in race and manners, language and culture; and, after reducing the Scots to utter servitude, they admit only Frenchmen to their friendship and service.

It was William Wallace and Robert the Bruce who finally pulled Scotland away from England, but their leadership didn't set a long-lasting example. Bruce's own son, David II (1324–71), invaded England, got captured, and was returned in exchange for a huge yearly ransom. While the Scottish peasants slaved to raise the money, David spent it on luxuries. Then he made an astonishing deal with Edward III. If Edward forgot about the ransom and David produced no heirs, England would receive the Scots crown. The Scots had put up with a lot from their kings, but this was a bit much. They carried on paying and, when David died childless, the throne went to the Scottish Stuart family.

The Stuarts, as well as being Scotland's most famous Royals, are also their best loved – considered to be sage and merciful rulers.

Well. They had their good moments.

In the main, the Stuarts did provide stability in Scotland, though they spent a large amount of time fighting their own self-seeking nobles. Whenever there was a hiatus in this civil unrest, the Stuarts filled it by trying to expand their kingdom into England in the south or the Highlands in the north.

When James VI of Scotland (1566–1625) succeeded to the English throne, the Scots monarchs had finally got what they wanted. The King of Scotland now ruled England and the Scots worshipped the ground he walked on.

James promptly left for London and never came back.

Living a life of comfort in London, the Stuarts' only real concern with Scotland was the fact that it was now Presbyterian. Rather than leaving well alone, they set about imposing their religion on their unfortunate northern subjects.

Even when the Scots Covenanters rebelled against Charles I

(1600–49), it was only to keep their religion, not to get rid of their king. When Charles was beheaded by Oliver Cromwell, the Covenanters obstinately backed his son. Once in power, Charles II set about wiping out the very people who had crowned him, killing thousands of his own subjects.

In the end the Stuart kings were ousted in 1688 and replaced by William of Orange and his wife Mary – a line of royalty that remains to this day.

Even then the Scots' doomed efforts were not over. The highlanders made several futile attempts to put the Stuarts back on the throne, despite none of the Stuart kings, from James VI and I onward, ever having returned to Scotland – and the fact that the only time they had concerned themselves with the Highlands was when they wanted to subdue it.

William and Mary had no interest in the Highlands either. Their dynasty preferred the northern Scots as far away as possible – though their land was desirable as a place to hunt and fish in.

An attitude that many feel persists to this day.

THE PRINCE OF THIEVES

For I resolved to spare no strain to drive out of this country every single Englishman; and had I not been met at every turn by the opposition of our nobles, 'tis beyond a doubt that I would have done it.
WILLIAM WALLACE (TO ROBERT THE BRUCE AFTER THE BATTLE OF FALKIRK)

Sir William Wallace (1270–1305) is considered Scotland's greatest hero, his reputation now overshadowing the previous titleholder, Robert the Bruce. Yet this is almost entirely due to the Oscar-winning movie *Braveheart* – before the film came out, most Scots couldn't tell you very much about William Wallace. Now he is famous across the world.

Yet one of the most fascinating aspects of the Wallace story is still largely unknown.

But first, it is necessary to quickly tell the established story.

With the sudden ending of the Canmore line, it was open season for the throne of Scotland – 13 different claimants insisted they should take over as king and fortress building became a national pastime.

In order to stave off all-out civil war, the Scots allowed Edward I of England to pick their king. Edward 'Longshanks' agreed, but insisted that whomever he picked must acknowledge him as their overlord. All 13 claimants agreed, naturally, since it gave them a better chance of being chosen. Edward was certainly no fool.

After hundreds of years of cross-border fighting, the Scots handed over their country lock, stock and barrel. Perhaps the new Scottish monarch, John Balliol (1249–1313), realised this – or perhaps he simply had no intention of keeping his word. Whatever the reason, he rebelled against England and Edward crushed him with ease. Longshanks then cut out the middleman by occupying Scotland with his own troops.

It had taken Edward 10 years of hard fighting to subdue the Briton tribes of Wales. He conquered feudal Scotland in five months.

Longshanks had taken over Scotland on principle, not because he wanted it, and despised the easy way its people had given in. The English soldiers, judges and tax collectors felt the same and treated the natives with violence and contempt.

However, the Scots have always been a perverse breed. They had taken years of abuse from their own rulers, but taxation by England was more than they could stomach. Edward raised more animosity in Scotland in a few months than neglectful Scots kings had managed in centuries.

That's when William Wallace appeared on the scene. The Wallaces were Britons from Wales who had settled in Strathclyde – indeed, the name means 'the Welshman'. Wallace and his father, Sir Malcolm, were knights thought too unimportant even to be summoned to swear allegiance to Edward. So they never did.

The fortunes of the Wallace family took a severe dip at the end of the thirteenth century. In 1291 Wallace's father was killed in a skirmish and Wallace was outlawed later, after getting into a fight with a group of English soldiers. Some accounts say the troops were molesting Wallace's wife, though there is no proof that he ever married. Resisting attempts at arrest, Wallace killed Hazelrig, the English Sheriff of Lanark, and was branded an outlaw. With nothing left to lose, he set about rallying the Scots, with the intention of destroying English oppression and returning the exiled Balliol to the throne.

In 1297 he faced an English army four times the size of his own at Stirling Bridge. The military genius of Wallace is often cited as the reason for the Scots' great victory that day. In fact, Wallace was only co-commander. His friend Andrew de Moray – leader of revolts further north – was equally in charge. Another overriding factor in the Scots victory was the arrogance of the English commanders, a haughtiness which caused them to make some monumental tactical blunders.

Wallace, waiting in the trees, must have thought Christmas had come early when the English began moving across the narrow Stirling Bridge. When the southern troops were split on either side of the river, Wallace attacked.

As the Scots broke cover and headed down the hill, an English knight, with the unflattering name of Marmaduke Twenge, led a cavalry charge uphill – ending on the ends of the Scottish pikes. Meanwhile the Scots archers, though few in number, were shooting downhill at a plainly visible target and having a fine time. Wallace and his cavalry hurtled through the midst of the English army, while his reserves crossed a ford (which the English had been too proud to bother with) and attacked from the rear.

Many English knights were forced into the river, where they discovered the disadvantages of trying to swim wearing 170lb of steel plate. Any troops who could still escape fled, and the ensuing manhunt created so many English corpses that they caused a small plague. The body of Hugh de Cressingham, a particularly hated English knight, was cut into little bits and sent across the country – a grisly beginning to the Scottish souvenir industry.

Wallace himself tastefully adorned his sword belt with de Cressingham's skin.

Snarling at the defeat, Edward I sent another gigantic army north. Wallace would happily have stuck to guerrilla tactics – but he was now the Guardian of Scotland and leading powerful nobles who didn't much like the idea of living rough in the woods for months. Reluctantly he mustered all the men he could and, once again, faced a vastly superior army – this time at Falkirk.

Wallace was now without Andrew de Moray, who had died from wounds he received at Stirling Bridge. Worse, he was supported by nobles who secretly objected to being led by a 'commoner'. Wallace had planned a surprise night attack, but two of his own barons, the Earl of Angus and the Earl of Dunbar, rode to the English camp and alerted Edward.

Realising that the surprise had been lost, Wallace deployed his army in the traditional three 'schiltrons' or columns, with their pikes pointing out. Then he waited.

The first wave of English cavalry floundered in the marshland as the Scots had hoped, and were picked off by archers. The second wave got through only to find they were galloping onto the unflinching 18-foot pikes. Wallace himself was inspiring his men no end, swinging a 6' 6" broadsword that could cut a war horse virtually in half. Though it had appeared inconceivable, it looked like the Scots might actually be victorious.

Then a second act of astonishing treachery occurred. The Scottish horsemen, who should have now destroyed the English archers, wheeled round and rode away. The aristocracy – who made up most of the cavalry – simply couldn't accept another victory by a man of low standing, who would then become irrefutably their superior.

Wallace fought on, surrounded by the men who had stayed true to him – and the Scots disappeared under a hail of arrows. Eventually, they were sheltering behind a wall of their own dead and Wallace had to be dragged, still fighting, from the battlefield. He was forced onto a horse so punctured with arrows that it died as it galloped away.

He was never to raise another army and, in shame, resigned his post as Guardian. After futile attempts to raise military help on the continent, he returned to Scotland and yet more betrayal. The new Guardians of Scotland – including Robert the Bruce – handed him over to the English. He was hung, drawn and quartered for treason, which was a bit ironic – he was one of the few who had never actually sworn fealty to Edward.

So how close was the real Wallace to his famous film portrayal in the Oscar-winning *Braveheart*? There are no paintings of the great warrior but, by all accounts, he was a handsome man. He was also gigantic – at least 6' 6" – quite an impressive sight in a country where the average height of a man was a little over five feet. For a great leader he was also very young – just 35 when he died.

There goes the Mel Gibson image.

And when Wallace died, the Queen of England was a young child, so their passionate relationship, portrayed in the film, is highly unlikely.

As for Edward I of England, he was neither a tyrant nor a butcher but simply a shrewd and powerful leader. Scotland had acknowledged him as its overlord – he was simply determined to make sure they stuck to their word. He may have been exceptionally brutal about it, but that brutality was easily matched by the Scots – including Wallace himself.

There is, however, another fascinating side to the Wallace story. If you look carefully at his life, comparisons with one of the most famous characters in British folklore become unavoidable.

Wallace was a minor knight who became a national hero. He was outlawed for killing an English sheriff. He lived in hiding in a forest (Legland Woods, on the banks of the river Ayr, was a favourite refuge). From these woods he attacked and looted convoys. Many of his targets carried English taxes that were crippling the poor and Wallace ensured the loyalty of the common people by sharing his spoils with them. He fought against an unpopular king while his own king was incarcerated abroad.

There is no denying that this is a perfect description of Robin Hood.

Not only the known facts, but also the legends about Wallace fit the story of Robin Hood. When Wallace was growing up in Dundee, the castle was under the control of an English constable named Selby. In 1291, Wallace killed Selby's son in a fight. The quarrel apparently started because Selby's comrades were mocking Wallace's bright green clothes.

Wallace is supposed to have fallen in love with the 18-year-old well-to-do daughter of Hugh Braidfute of Lamington. Because Wallace was an outlaw they could not marry. Instead, they carried on a clandestine affair until she was murdered. Her name was Marion Braidfute.

One of Wallace's comrades in arms was a man named Edward Little. Wallace was a truly enormous man and he had a smaller brother called John. When you combine these factors, it isn't hard to see where 'Little John', Robin Hood's right-hand man, came from. Wallace was also joined by his old friend John Blair, a Benedictine monk, surely the inspiration for 'Friar Tuck'.

Robin Hood is supposed to have lived near Nottingham during the reign of the English King John. John ruled a century before Wallace was ever born; yet tales of a legendary English outlaw only became popular after Wallace's death — and the name 'Robin' does not appear until long after that.

The story of William Wallace was simply too stirring not to be retold. But, as happened so often, England was vastly more powerful than Scotland – and to the victor go the spoils. English chroniclers couldn't admit that an outstandingly noble, brave and selfless hero was some rebel Scot – it would be perfect propaganda for the aggressive northerners.

So Scotland's hero was made into an English legend instead.

William Wallace *was* famous long before *Braveheart*. Just under a different name.

ROBERT THE BRUCE

There are few more impressive sights in the world than a Scotsman on the make.

J.M. BARRIE (1860-1937), *WHAT EVERY WOMAN KNOWS*

Robert the Bruce (1274–1329) has, for generations, been venerated as Scotland's greatest hero – his story is well known to all schoolchildren and, after almost 700 years, still generates a sense of national pride. Edward I, 'Hammer of the Scots', had conquered the country and the people lived in fear of his tyranny. Robert the Bruce rallied his people and tried to win back Scotland's independence. The brave Scots tried and tried again to overthrow their mighty neighbour, but the English armies were just too large and Bruce was forced to go on the run.

Then one day, hiding in a cave and lamenting the fate of his people, Bruce saw a spider hanging by one thread near the cave entrance. The spider was trying to climb to the roof, but every time it neared its destination, it slipped back down again. Over and over again the spider climbed and fell, climbed and fell until, finally, it reached the top.

'If that wee spider can display such tenacity and achieve its goal despite overwhelming odds, then so can I,' said the Bruce, to nobody in particular. He went out, raised another army and threw the English out of Scotland.

It's a nice story and illustrates Scotland's dilemma very well but, unfortunately, Sir Walter Scott made it up in the nineteenth century.

What isn't in dispute is the fact that Robert the Bruce won Scotland its independence, where his rebellious predecessor William Wallace failed. As such, Bruce and not Wallace became the national hero – and underwent the customary character whitewash that comes with victory.

Ironically, this idealistic depiction of Bruce as righteous indignation in armour has altered thanks to the American film industry – not exactly famed for its historical accuracy. The film *Braveheart*, however, portrayed William Wallace as the truly virtuous force in Scotland's fight for independence – and presented the world with a Robert the Bruce who was flawed and weak in comparison to Wallace.

It's unlike Hollywood to give a realistic portrayal of any historical character but, for once, the film could lay claim to a view more valid than that of many history books. Robert the Bruce wasn't just flawed – in many ways he was downright nasty. But it wasn't until a major movie portrayed him as less than perfect that the chinks in his heroic armour became public knowledge.

The same is true, incidentally, of the reputation of Edward I – arch enemy of Bruce and Wallace. Though Scots historians have, naturally, frowned upon Edward's policy of rape and pillage in their country, he remained popular in England as Edward Longshanks, the Crusader Prince. Thanks, once again, to *Braveheart*, the popular public conception of Edward has changed, correctly or not, to one of a vicious tyrant with a distinctly odd family life. Such is the power of celluloid in the myth-making process.

But back to Robert the Bruce. Was he really the country's great and noble saviour – the 'Good King Robert' of Scots history? And, if not, how did he manage to hold the position of *the* Scots hero for so long? And what other long cherished perceptions about Robert the Bruce are less than accurate?

Robert de Brus was a French-speaking noble descended from a line of Norman feudal lords who had only recently settled in Scotland. As such, it can be argued that concern for the native population was not at the forefront of his mind. His desire to rule them, however, was a different matter altogether.

Robert the Bruce did have a reasonable claim to the Scottish throne. His grandfather, also Robert, had been one of 13 contenders for King of Scotland when King Alexander III and his heir, Margaret, unexpectedly died.

The Bruces had never supported John Balliol, Edward Longshanks' choice for the King of Scotland and, when Balliol rebelled, they swore loyalty to the English king. This was a logical, if unpatriotic, move. If Edward were to pick a new Scots king, the Bruce line now stood a much better chance. At this point, however, Edward I wasn't putting too much store in the loyalty of would-be Scots kings, and occupied Scotland himself.

William Wallace, who had never taken the fealty oath, now emerged to lead the fight for Scotland's independence – his intention being to return Balliol to the throne. In Wallace's mind, Balliol was Scotland's rightful king, whatever his flaws.

Robert the Bruce had no desire to help Wallace – the return of a rival line to the Scots throne definitely did not suit his personal agenda. Besides, Bruce's name was on the 'Ragman's Roll' – the list of those who had sworn loyalty to Edward – and Edward obviously did not take the breaking of that oath lightly. To make matters worse, Bruce was the Earl of Carrick and his father was Governor of Carlisle.

If he joined the fight for Scottish independence, Robert the Bruce had an awful lot to lose.

On the other hand, if the Scottish uprising succeeded, it wouldn't help Bruce's goal of kingship to be seen fighting for the opposition. So, the first time Edward called upon him to put down a Scots uprising, Bruce took a chance, gathered his men together, and promptly joined the Scots side. Even if a spirit of genuine patriotism was motivating Bruce, he was still no supporter of John Balliol and there was suspicion among some nobles as to why exactly he was there.

In the end, this particular revolt didn't turn out to be a glorious fight for freedom – the English army turned out to be a lot bigger than the Scots expected and they negotiated for peace instead. Bruce wasn't imprisoned, but it would be fair to say Edward had partially lost confidence in him, and that his political position in England was now weakened.

Then Wallace defeated the English at Stirling Bridge – a tremendous victory that galvanised the Scots and made independence a distinct possibility once more. Wallace became Guardian of Scotland, a living legend, and Bruce was suddenly back on board.

The euphoria didn't last long. At the battle of Falkirk, the Scots were soundly defeated and the guardianship of Scotland fell to Bruce and another noble, John Comyn.

Comyn, like Wallace, was committed to returning Balliol to the throne and had a valid claim to the throne himself. Bruce still refused to accept Balliol as monarch and believed that his own line should rule Scotland. It was a pairing doomed to failure. At one point Comyn became so peeved with Bruce that he publicly grabbed him by the throat.

Robert the Bruce realised he was being edged out of the picture by Balliol's supporters, and that his chance of becoming king was slipping away. If Balliol regained the Scottish throne, Bruce might well become a non-entity. This was a situation he wasn't going to put up with. While Comyn and Wallace fought on, he emerged from hiding and surrendered to Edward I.

Edward knew that Bruce was more useful as an ally than a prisoner and neither man wanted Balliol back on the Scottish throne. In 1303, when Edward marched into Scotland once more, Robert the Bruce was at his side. On the order of the English king, Bruce led an unsuccessful raid to capture William Wallace and supplied siege engines for an attack on Stirling Castle.

The Scots were no match for Edward's might. John Comyn negotiated terms and managed to retain a position of power as part of a 'Scottish Council' – answerable, of course, to Edward. Bruce, back in Edward's good books, got a place on the Council too – and things were back to normal. Only William Wallace fought on. In the eyes of the Council, however, Wallace had outlived his usefulness. In a shameful act of betrayal, they handed Scotland's greatest hero over to Edward, who executed him in London.

England was now the outright master of Scotland and John Balliol was further than ever from regaining his throne. This was an impossible state of affairs for John Comyn, who still plotted and planned to remove Edward Longshanks from his country. Even if he couldn't get Balliol back, he held a valid claim to the throne himself. Further rebellion also held definite advantages for Robert the Bruce, whose father had recently died.

Now, not just the Bruce line, but Robert himself might rule an independent Scotland.

Comyn and Bruce entered into a secret conspiracy to rise against England once more. What agreement, if any, the plotters reached is uncertain. It may be the case that Bruce proposed an alliance and that Comyn turned him down. There is also some evidence that Comyn informed Edward I of Bruce's intentions, in order to force his rival's hand – an opinion Bruce himself voiced more than once.

If this was the case, it was a clever trick. When Edward became aware of Bruce's rebellious intentions, the latter was forced to flee north to avoid execution.

Now there was no turning back. If he hoped ever to have real power, Robert the Bruce, like it or not, was committed to the Scottish cause.

Bruce asked Comyn to meet him at the Church of the Grey Friars in Dumfries, to either have it out with him or figure out what to do next. The fact that Comyn agreed to the encounter at all suggests he had not betrayed Bruce. Then again, meeting on sacred ground was normally a fair insurance against violence.

Not this time. Whatever passed between the two men in the churchyard that night led Bruce to stab John Comyn. Bruce always maintained his regret at killing another human on hallowed ground and insisted the murder was done in the heat of a rage at Comyn's treachery. However, the fact that John Comyn was only wounded, and that he was on hallowed ground, didn't stop Bruce from allowing his companions to go back and finish him off.

Whatever the reasons, Comyn's death removed Bruce's only serious obstacle to crowning himself King of Scotland.

With his bridges well and truly burned, Bruce acted with a speed that suggested Comyn's death might not have been as accidental as he later insisted. He had surprise on his side, but the ease with which he sacked the English installations and gathered followers as he marched on Scone, suggests some measure of preparation. It's hard not to wonder if the churchyard killing was the first step in a pre-planned assault on the Crown of Scotland – which would make Comyn's death premeditated murder. But Bruce had reached Scone and crowned himself before any of Comyn's or Balliol's supporters had time to object.

Robert the Bruce had not become monarch by using the strength, right or courage which history has attributed to him. He gained the throne through duplicity, selfishness and naked ambition.

So how did he manage to become such a national hero?

Bruce might have used all his worst qualities to get the Scottish throne, but he also used his best. The ability to judge accurately when to switch sides displayed Bruce's intelligence and ingenuity. The fact that he could get away with it indicates significant charm. His tenacity meant he never faltered in pursuit of his goal. Good or bad, Robert the Bruce possessed quite a barrage of social weapons. He would have to use all of them in his coming trials, and the fact that he succeeded where most men would have surely failed is what has helped cement his heroic reputation.

Bruce was King of Scotland, but his struggle had barely begun. He had hoped for European acknowledgement of his claim but, instead, was excommunicated by the Pope for murdering Comyn on sacred ground. Scotland was still an occupied country and Edward, incensed by Bruce's actions, had started preparation for yet another rampage north. Bruce had innumerable enemies in Scotland – the Comyn clan certainly weren't too fond of him – and he wasn't getting nearly as much support as he had hoped.

In his first major skirmish with an English force, Bruce lost and his captured knights were executed as outlaws rather than being ransomed. This was not the done thing in these days and showed just how furious Edward Longshanks felt at Bruce's latest 'betrayal'. The other Scots nobles avoided him like the plague – it was just too dangerous to be on the new monarch's side – and nobody felt he would be King much longer anyway.

Within a few months of being crowned, Bruce was a fugitive with only a tiny band of supporters, his fortunes at a lower ebb than they had ever been.

This was not a situation Bruce could lie or cheat his way out of, so now his better qualities came to the fore. He refused to give in. His charm and indomitable spirit inspired his men and his following slowly grew. He revealed real talent for military strategy, conducting a successful guerrilla war then openly attacking English forces. As the King of Scotland's star rose, the legends of his prowess, cunning and goodness began to mount – Scott's spider story comes from this period in Bruce's life. The following passage, written in 1308 by a pro-English Scot to an English official, shows how much Bruce's image was being enhanced by self-propaganda.

> I hear that Bruce never had the good will of his own followers or the people generally so much with him as now. It appears that God is with him . . . the people believe that Bruce will carry all before him . . . exhorted by false preachers from Bruce's army. For these preachers have told the people that they have found a prophecy of Merlin, that after the death of Le Roy Coveytous [Edward I] the people of Scotland and Wales shall band together and have full lordship and live in peace together to the end of the world.

This gives a pretty good clue to where Robert the Bruce, the legend, begins. It begins, to some extent, with Bruce himself. Medieval spin-doctoring was another of his many talents.

The rest, as they say, is history – the famous part of the Bruce story. Edward I died and his son, though not the effeminate weakling history has branded him, had neither the awesome presence nor the military skill of his father. In 1314, Bruce's growing army defeated a far superior English force at Bannockburn and the Scots drafted the *Declaration of Arbroath*, a splendidly worded assertion of their independence.

Edward II, to his credit, never gave up the struggle against Bruce. It wasn't until he was finally deposed that his son, Edward III, acknowledged Scotland as a separate nation. Bruce lived just long enough to see his lifelong ambition fulfilled. Scotland was independent and he was finally king of a real country, not just a satellite state.

That, in the end, is Robert the Bruce's true claim to national adoration – the freeing of Scotland from oppression against overwhelming odds. He was not as great a man as Wallace, or even John Comyn, if greatness entails sticking to principles, honesty and loyalty. On the other hand, he won and Wallace and Comyn didn't. And to be honest, for the times in which Bruce lived, he needed those bad qualities to achieve victory as much as he needed the good ones.

And still the legends grow. It has often been asserted that the *Declaration of Arbroath* is the basis of the American Constitution and there is some truth in this. The *Declaration of Arbroath*, however, formed the basis for a much more sinister union and another Scottish document entirely became far more influential in shaping the American Constitution. But we will come to those in another chapter.

One final twist in the legend of Robert the Bruce is worth mentioning. In recent years it has become accepted that Bruce died of leprosy –

another image reinforced by the film *Braveheart*. In his later years he did develop a severe skin disease and his health suffered greatly. Bruce himself swore that his sickness was a punishment from God for his churchyard sin and leprosy was an appropriately terrible price. However, John Barbour, who chronicled the King's life in *The Brus* (1375), puts his ill health down to a life of campaigning. Bruce's own doctors did not diagnose him with leprosy, nor was he separated from his family, courtiers or nobles. In fact, he gathered quite a crowd on his deathbed.

And no wonder.

He was, after all, Scotland's greatest hero.

ENGLAND, MY ENGLAND

At school we were brought up on tales of Bruce, Wallace and Burns. They were the greatest. Our village was the greatest. Our school was the greatest. And the English were vilified. We thought England was our enemy and the English were poison.

BILL SHANKLY (1913–81), FOOTBALL PLAYER AND MANAGER, *THE ONLY GAME*

Scotland has a reputation for being the underdog. For most of the country's history it has had a large aggressive neighbour in the shape of England, a country neighbour who dearly wanted to annex, conquer or annihilate the Scots, whichever happened to be easiest.

In fact, the opposite is true. For most of recorded history, England has had little desire to invade Scotland, and certainly no inclination to own it. The Scots, on the other hand, have done their level best to seize English land every chance they got. Failing that, they have satisfied themselves with centuries of rape and pillage south of the border.

In its earliest incarnations, of course, there was no question of Scotland attacking anybody. The entire country was divided into tribal factions, each happily occupied with fighting each other. A heady mixture of Scandinavians, Picts, Scots and Angles battled it out with one another before gradually congealing into a volatile, unstable nation.

In a sense, these tribes were invaders themselves, arriving from other lands and staking out areas of Scotland for their own. Once they became some sort of nation, they naturally looked around for somewhere new to invade. Since Scotland was surrounded by water on its other three sides, England was the obvious choice for expansion.

In its formative years, Scotland itself suffered one major attempt at occupation. It was invaded by the armies of Rome. The remote desolation of northern Scotland wasn't exactly a major prize, but the Roman Empire was in the process of conquering the world, and couldn't leave a bit out just because it was inhospitable. It was at first thought that the Roman attempt at conquering Scotland was an English invasion – however, the Romans only came from that direction because they had conquered England first.

In a fair fight, the trained legionnaires could easily defeat the northern natives, but they couldn't triumph over guerrilla tactics on forbidding heather-clad terrain. Instead, the Romans retreated into England, building Hadrian's Wall as a barrier between themselves and the savage northerners.

Left to their own devices, the Celtic tribes of Scotland ventured down to the wall, launched surprise raids, plundered their richer neighbours and escaped back into the wilderness.

And set a precedent that lasted over a millennium and a half.

Kenneth MacAlpin (d.858) took the invading business to new heights. Having united enough of Scotland to call it a nation, he undertook no less than six separate forays into the south. A whole line of Alpin kings followed his lead with a persistence which was quite awe-inspiring, considering that they constantly had to defend their own territory from Danish and Scandinavian attacks in the north and west. From 877 AD to 1040, Scotland and northern England battled back and forth, peppering their hostilities with uneasy truces. But, in the end, the sheer persistence of the Scots won out and the English border was forced farther and farther south. By the reign of Malcolm II (1005–1034), Scotland extended all the way down to Lancashire – the largest the country would ever be.

In 1057 the English spectacularly got their own back, providing men and money for an invasion of Scotland, then ruled by the infamous MacBeth. But this wasn't an English invasion either – it was led by the exiled Scot Malcolm Canmore who considered himself to be Scotland's true king. The English king, Edward the Confessor, didn't want Scotland for himself, but he figured Canmore's gratitude ought to be worth something. He should have known better. On becoming Malcolm III, Canmore turned round and invaded England.

But the south was now ruled by the powerful Norman king, William the Conqueror, who marched back up and forced Malcolm to swear loyalty. Revitalised by an influx of Anglo-Norman dissenters, Malcolm invaded England again and was killed for his efforts.

Under the house of Canmore, the massive infusion of southern Anglo-Normans turned Scotland into little more than an English vassal state. Again, this was no invasion. The Canmore kings had invited the southerners in.

Once each wave of Anglo-Normans felt themselves to be suitably Scottish, they turned around and helped invade the south. Time and time again the raiders were repulsed and made to pay homage to England. They swore fealty so often that England, naturally, ended up considering Scotland to be its property.

The situation got so bad that when the Canmore line ended, the Scots nobles actually *invited* Edward I of England to pick their next king. Edward selected John Balliol and expected a bit of appreciation for it. He didn't want Scotland either, but he did want Scots troops to help him fight the French. Balliol, true to form, formed an alliance with France instead.

Edward Longshanks had the ultimate no-nonsense approach to the matter. He had picked a king. That king, and his nobles, had sworn allegiance. They went back on their word and Edward just wasn't having it. He marched into Scotland, captured Balliol, burned a few towns, set up military outposts and appointed English judiciaries to collect taxes. He then left with the Stone of Destiny, on which Scottish monarchs were traditionally crowned. For the first time, the Scots were the victims of neighbourly oppression – and they didn't like it one little bit.

The Scots army was usually little more than a rabble led by self-seeking nobles or tribal leaders. Though lowland Scots peasants fought with great bravery and the highlanders with unrivalled savagery, they rarely stood a chance of beating the English, who had the finest army in the world. But freedom is, indeed, a powerful battle cry. Both William Wallace and Robert the Bruce managed the unthinkable feat of defeating larger English armies and eventually secured liberty for their country.

It is this period in Scottish history which forged the enduring picture of a smaller nation fighting fiercely for independence. Yet these events, heralded by the Scots own inability to lead themselves, took place over about 30 years, with nobles like Robert the Bruce changing sides frequently. And when the next invasion from England came, it was again led by a Scot. Edward Balliol (c.1283–1364), son of John, led an English army north, claiming to be the true king of Scotland.

Talk about history repeating itself.

Balliol lasted no longer than his father. Bruce's son, David II (1324–71), took back his father's throne and, you guessed it, launched an attack on England. He was beaten, captured and ransomed back to Scotland.

In the period that followed, the Bruce line was succeeded by the Stuart kings and England was allowed a bit of breathing space. Under a trio of weak monarchs, the Scots went back to fighting each other and the English went back to building up their military might for use against the country they really did want to conquer – France.

It took a strong Stuart king, James I (1394–1437), to restore order to Scotland – and his own nobles killed him for the effort – but at least the Scots resembled a nation again. James II (1430–60) then led the unified Scots on a foray south in an attempt to gain some advantage from the English 'Wars of the Roses' and died when the cannon he was inspecting blew up.

Again, the country was plunged into chaos and James III (1452–88) died trying to sort it out. Again a coherent nation re-emerged under James IV (1473–1513). James then allied himself with the French, took the largest Scots army of all time and, surprise, surprise, invaded England. In 1513 the army was annihilated at Flodden, and James IV was killed.

Totally failing to learn from his father's mistakes, James V (1512–42) allied himself with the French too. The English, seeing Scotland as a potential French stronghold on their doorstep, declared war and the Scots were easily defeated at the battle of Solway Moss.

The Scottish–French alliance was getting far too serious for the English. They didn't want the trouble of trying to conquer this annoying, aggressive country but they couldn't let Scotland become a launching pad for a French invasion.

Henry VIII of England came up with a simple solution – his son would marry James V's infant daughter, Mary (Queen of Scots) and create an English alliance instead. When the Scots proved less than enthusiastic, he burned and pillaged his way north, in what became known as the 'Rough Wooing', but gave up when Mary escaped to France and didn't return until she was an adult.

Mary Queen of Scots (1542–87) was an enigmatic figure. She never showed a great inclination to invade the south and it is popularly believed that she was too flighty and too unstable to properly wield her power. Perhaps. But there is also evidence that Mary's lack of military action was due to a sneaky new takeover strategy. Already a strong contender to inherit the English throne, her marriage to the boorish Lord Darnley strengthened her position.

Elizabeth I of England found Mary threatening enough to imprison her for 17 years and then execute her – but the Queen of Scots' ploy worked in long run. Her son James VI (1566–1625) succeeded Elizabeth to become the first king of Britain. Now the Scots would never have to invade again.

But why break the habit of a lifetime? In 1639 and 1640 the Scottish Covenanters rose against Charles I (1600–49) of Britain. Though their original intention was to thwart Charles's attempts to inflict Episcopalian religion on their country, they soon saw a chance to do some imposing of their own. In return for Oliver Cromwell's promise to make Scots Presbyterianism the religion of England too, they came south to fight Charles on his own ground.

When the English went too far and executed Charles I, the Scots promptly declared his son Charles II (1630–85) king, and invaded England yet again. England's new leader, Oliver Cromwell, wiped them out and marched north in retaliation.

Cromwell's occupation is the only period in history when Scotland was truly subdued – largely because Cromwell was enforcing religious principles, not taking land – and there were those in Scotland who were not adverse to Cromwell's puritanical stance. But an occupation is an occupation and when Cromwell died and Charles II finally became king, the Scots were delighted.

But the Stuart dynasty was on its last legs. Charles II had possessed a certain brutal charm, but James VII (1633–1701) was as unpopular as Charles I had been. He, too, lost the British throne.

Then it was the turn of the Scottish highlanders to invade, launching a series of campaigns to try and put the Stuarts back in power. In 1745 the highlanders made their last foray south and, astonishingly, got further than the Scots ever had in their history. But, 123 miles from London, they finally realised that Scotland's dream – the conquest of England – was never going to become a reality. They turned back and were annihilated at Culloden Moor – the last battle fought on British soil.

Scotland was never a peaceable little realm fighting to remain independent from a powerful, avaricious neighbour, though that's the way the nation is portrayed in legend, book and film. The Scots were a small, aggressive nation, well aware that their neighbour was richer than they were. With the dogged determination that characterised so many Scottish enterprises, they set out to try and take that wealth, despite the fact that they were outmanned, outgunned, outplanned and outclassed.

It's not the way the Scots like to see their relationship with the 'Auld Enemy' – but you have to admire their persistence.

THE FORGOTTEN JOURNEY OF HENRY SINCLAIR

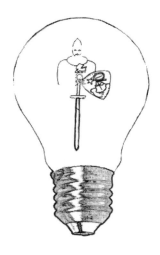

> As the sea ran high and we did not know what country it was, we were afraid at first to approach it, but by God's blessing the wind lulled, and then there came a great calm. Some of the crew pulled ashore and soon returned with great joy with news that they had found an excellent country and a still better harbour.
>
> ANTONIO ZENO, ADMIRAL TO HENRY SINCLAIR, WRITING TO HIS BROTHER

It is no secret that Christopher Columbus didn't really discover America – for a start, there were plenty of people already living in the New World when he got there. Columbus wasn't even the first white man to reach America. It is generally accepted that Viking longships crossed the Atlantic long before Columbus was born.

Though there is no tangible evidence, there are also legends of Irish, Norse, Breton, Basque, Portuguese and Scots fishermen reaching the North American coast.

If these legends are true, then the New World was getting pretty old by the time Christopher Columbus reached it. The question is, did these early working mariners actually reach America? Is it possible that they were lying, boasting or just plain mistaken?

There is proof that one crossing did take place – and took place a century before the voyage of Columbus. This navigator reached North America and explored what is now Newfoundland, Canada and the USA. He did not have the financial backing or the support of royalty – nor was he under the misapprehension that he was heading for China. This man knew exactly what he was looking for.

His name was Henry Sinclair.

Henry Sinclair, son of Sir William Sinclair, was born in Rosslyn Castle in 1345. When he was 13 years old, his father died fighting in the crusades, and Henry became Baron of Rosslyn while little more than a boy. He must have grown into a reliable and resourceful man, however, for King Hakkon of Norway, who ruled over tracts of land in the north of Scotland, eventually offered him the title of Earl of Orkney.

There was a catch. Orkney hadn't had an effective ruler for many years and the island had degenerated into lawlessness. To reap the benefits of Earldom, Sinclair would have to restore order. He left his home and friends in wooded Roslin and set off for the treeless islands of Orkney. He was 33 years old.

Henry had taken on quite a task. The Orkney Islands were raided by mainland Scots and patrolled by pirates and smugglers. Most Orkneymen were contemptuous of King Hakkon's laws and felt Norway was too far away to enforce its will on them.

To police an island community Sinclair had to have ships – but building boats was difficult on islands that didn't have trees. Undaunted, Sinclair constructed a base, Kirkwall Castle, and imported wood from his Rosslyn Barony until he had an impressive battle fleet of 13 vessels.

Henry Sinclair seems to have been a good ruler and certainly gained the respect of the Orkney Islanders. As he got to know the inhabitants, he began to hear their tales – tales which, naturally, tended to feature the sea. There were stories of sea serpents longer than ships, of giant whirlpools, of islands that sank and rose – with tales like that it was a wonder Henry Sinclair ever set foot in a boat. But Sinclair also heard legends of fishermen sailing in search of better catches and reaching islands they didn't recognise. He listened to stories of the dreaded Vik-men (Vikings), who had discovered not only new islands, but vast lands over the western sea.

Henry was beginning to get some first-hand experience of sailing himself. His allegiance to the Norwegians meant he sometimes sailed to state events in Scandinavia, but this kind of navigation was small potatoes compared to the journey he would soon undertake.

Having successfully brought the Orkneys to order, Sinclair turned his attention to the unruly Shetland Islands, also part of his domain. Around 1390, his fleet set sail for what amounted to a full-scale invasion.

On this short journey, a chance event would change Henry Sinclair's life. His fleet stopped at Fer Island, notorious for offshore reefs and unpredictable currents – but Sinclair wanted to make sure everyone got the message that he was in charge. He landed with a large group of men and began to make his position clear to the gathered islanders. Suddenly they snatched up their weapons and began to run for the shore.

There had been a shipwreck.

A ship running aground was like a lottery win for the islanders. On these tiny desolate islands, life was much harsher than on the mainland, and a broken ship could provide all manner of luxuries. The Shetlanders considered any grounded vessel to be theirs and had no qualms about killing the survivors to make sure it stayed that way.

To Henry's relief, the stranded ship was not one of his own. The unknown vessel was plainly breaking up, but its crew was reluctant to swim for shore while the inhabitants of Fer milled around the beach brandishing fish knives. Henry had his men drive the furious natives away and the stranded sailors were brought safely to land.

The Prince of the Orkneys was astonished to discover that the sinking ship was not Scots, Scandinavian or even Irish – it was Venetian. Sinclair's delight at finding a vessel from the famous seafaring city was compounded when he found that the captain was Nicolo Zeno, brother of the legendary naval hero Carlo Zeno – Carlo the Lion. Nicolo was accompanied by Antonio Zeno, who may also have been his brother, or possibly his son. The Zenos had been exploring the area when their ships were caught on the shoals of Fer Island.

Sinclair immediately invited Nicolo Zeno to join him; the Venetian's nautical expertise would prove invaluable on the Shetland campaign, especially his ability to build decent cannons. Sinclair easily took the Shetland Islands and, in return, granted Nicolo Zeno a knighthood. A fateful partnership was born.

The new nautical allies made voyages to Iceland, then to Greenland – both of which had small colonies on their coasts. Unfortunately, the cold climate proved too much for the ageing Nicolo who died in Greenland, but Antonio stayed and was made an Admiral of the Orkney fleet. Though only fragments survive, his letters to Carlo Zeno are vital evidence of Sinclair's upcoming feat.

It was at this point that a second momentous occurrence changed Henry Sinclair's life. A fisherman, missing for over two decades, suddenly turned up in the Orkneys claiming to have sailed clear across the Atlantic. Antonio, in one of his letters to Carlo the Lion, recounts the fisherman's tale.

> Six and twenty years ago four fishing boats put out to sea, and encountering a heavy storm, were driven over the sea in utter helplessness for many days; when at length, the tempest abating, they discovered an island called Estotiland, lying to the westwards more than 1000 leagues from Frisaland [presumably Fer Island].

The native population of this strange island (most likely Newfoundland, off the coast of Canada) spoke a language the sailors couldn't understand. The fishermen explored the island and concluded that it was a little smaller than Iceland (Newfoundland is almost identical in size to Iceland). The fisherman claimed that the natives traded with Greenland and had met westerners before. The chief even had Latin books in his possession, though neither he nor any of the natives could read them. The natives also told the fishermen of a land to the south.

> He says that towards the south there is a great and populous country, very rich in gold. They sow corn and make a drink of a kind that northern people take as we do wine. They have woods of immense extent.

The natives had 'insisted' that the fisherman stay but, eventually, the mariners were allowed to leave. They sailed south to see these 'great and populous' lands for themselves, but were met with hostility. A number of mariners were captured and killed before the captors realised that these white men had an astonishing skill. They were able to make fishing nets. Instantly, they went from being captives to captive guests, exhibited to other tribes for 13 years.

It is hard to guess where the fishermen ended up, though it may well have been as far south as Florida. In their description, they make reference to lands that may even be Mexico:

> The farther you go Southwest, however, the more refinement you meet with, because the climate is more temperate, and accordingly there they have cities and temples dedicated to their idols, in which they sacrifice men and afterwards eat them. In those parts they have some knowledge and use of Gold and Silver.

Eventually, some of the sailors escaped and made their way back to friendly Estotiland, where they traded for a while before finally sailing back to Orkney.

It is possible, of course, that this was one big fisherman's tale. Yet the story certainly isn't impossible. True or not, Henry Sinclair believed the account and made up his mind to see these fantastic new lands for himself.

Sinclair assembled part of his fleet and set sail. Antonio Zeno came too, and his letters recorded the endeavours to reach this 'New World' – the first time, incidentally, that the famous term was used.

Sinclair's fleet managed to cross the Atlantic without any apparent loss, heading west until they finally reached an island they did not recognise. One of the inhabitants spoke Icelandic and informed Sinclair that the island was called Icaria – a variation of Icarus (Icarus, son of Daedalus, features in ancient Scots and Irish mythology). What later translators of Zeno's letters called Estotiland was actually Escociland – land of Scots.

Sinclair had reached Newfoundland only to find it had a Celtic colony.

These colonists were not friendly, however, and Sinclair hurriedly sailed west again. Here he found yet another land, fertile and pleasant. Sinclair was so enthused with what he had discovered that he proposed establishing a settlement there and then.

His men were more cautious. Winter was not far off and, once it set in, they might well be stuck till the following summer. Sinclair saw their point. Keeping some rowboats and a few men, he sent the rest back, led by a reluctant Antonio.

There have been various doubts cast about exactly where Sinclair had got to at this point. Some believe that he was really in Greenland, but that simply cannot be. Greenland did not have trees, fertile soil and a climate 'mild and pleasant beyond description'. Besides, Greenland was fairly well known, especially to Henry Sinclair. Nor was this new land Newfoundland. Sinclair was using the fishermen who had already been to Newfoundland as guides – they did not recognise where they were. Admittedly, Antonio Zeno called the place where he parted from Sinclair an 'island' – but did so before Henry Sinclair had a chance to return and verify that the land was much larger.

Antonio's own descriptions of landmarks – like the giant 'smoking hole' eight days march from Sinclair's camp – were exhaustively followed up by the writer Fredrick J. Pohl. Pohl also analysed geographical, social and geological evidence, studied place names and collected Indian legends. After gathering a mass of relevant data, he came to the undeniable conclusion that Henry Sinclair had landed in Nova Scotia.

Sinclair had discovered the continent of North America.

Henry Sinclair waited out the winter before setting off again. During that year he explored inland and appears to have encountered the Micmac tribe of Nova Scotia. Micmac legends speak of a king with three daughters (Sinclair had three daughters), from an island across the sea, who landed with many soldiers, stayed for a year and then left.

While waiting for a good wind to take him home, Henry sailed south-west – a course that would take him along the coast of New England. On one of his last shore trips one of Sinclair's loyal knights died. The exact cause of his demise is not noted, but it would appear his passing was most definitely marked. In a place called Westford, Massachusetts, there is a rock with a strange motif imprinted on its surface – the weathering on the stone dates these markings at several centuries old. An image has been made by punching holes on the rock's surface. It shows an armoured head, a shield and a fourteenth century sword and pommel. Ian Moncrieff in *The Highland Clans* has identified the heraldic emblems on the shield as those of the Gunn clan. The Gunns were one of the tribes of Northern Scotland – and the vassals of the Sinclairs.

Henry Sinclair sailed uneventfully back across the Atlantic to land safely in Orkney in 1399, almost a hundred years before Columbus left. He was quick to tell everyone of the new land he had found and surely must have planned a return, or even an attempt at colonization.

It was never to happen. Only a year later, Henry IV of England raided Scotland and, from a base in Edinburgh, sailed up the coast and attacked Orkney. Henry Sinclair's normal common sense seems to have given way to fury. Despite being hopelessly outnumbered, he left the protection of Kirkwall Castle and launched an all-out attack. He died in battle, along with many of those who sailed the Atlantic with him. There would be no return journey.

Prince Henry Sinclair explored North America – a continent that Columbus never actually saw. He left proof of this in Indian legend, in the rocks of New England and in the letters of Antonio Zeno. If more evidence were needed, it came in 1849, when a cannon was dredged from the harbour of Louisburg on Cape Breton Island. Experts identified the gun as being a naval cannon, of late fourteenth century Venetian design.

So why isn't Henry Sinclair famous?

Publicity and opportunity seem to be the answer. Unlike Columbus, Sinclair didn't have the benefit of Royal backing, central European focus or a newly invented printing press to spread word of his exploits. He did not open up a route by which powerful European nations could pour into the New World, enslave its inhabitants and carry off its wealth. The great seafarer, Carlo Zeno, knew of his accomplishments, but Carlo lived in the Mediterranean. He seems to have made the mistake of thinking that America could only be reached by the long and torturous route of going via Scotland, Iceland, Greenland and Newfoundland – it may not have seemed worth the effort. His greatest mistake as a voyager was probably not realising it was possible to go straight across.

Columbus raised interest and money by claiming that the Atlantic was a short cut to the riches of the Orient. It wasn't until Europeans began to realise the New World actually offered greater opportunities than the East that everyone scrambled to get there. There is evidence, however, that Columbus himself had heard of Henry Sinclair's voyage. Before he set off for the west, he made an exploratory trip to Greenland.

Prince Henry's heirs showed none of their ancestor's enthusiasm for exploration, but obviously admired his efforts. In 1444 Sinclair's grandson, William, built a beautiful chapel at Rosslyn, which stands to this day. Inside are carvings of what can only be described as cactus and maize. Many scholars have refused to accept that these images, which predate Columbus, could possibly represent American vegetation. Yet Brian Moffat, an expert on ancient carvings, has confirmed that they do not correspond to any medieval interpretations of European plants.

Visitors to the chapel have long wondered how William Sinclair could possibly have known about American botany before Columbus discovered America.

Unless, of course, his grandfather had got there first.

As a race, the Scots were not a notable force in the exploration of the globe. They tended either to stay put or to migrate. They were not the type to look around for the sake of it and then come back – there was nothing in it for them. There are, of course, notable – if little known – exceptions. Captain James Cook (1728–99), one of the greatest explorers in history, had Scottish parents. John McDowall Stuart (1815–66) was the first person to cross Australia from south to north and Sir Charles Wylie Thomson (1830–82) was the first person to systematically explore the ocean depths.

But there are two areas where the Scots explorers had a huge effect on the world. The first is in the exploration of Northern America and the Arctic Regions.

The northern latitude of both Scotland and Canada – a land filled with Scots immigrants – made the Arctic an irresistible lure, if a frozen wasteland can ever be called irresistible. Then again, the Scots have always been used to bad weather.

Alexander McKenzie (1767–1820), the first white man to cross the North American continent, was born in the Outer Hebrides. Sir John Ross (1777–1856) was the first to explore thoroughly the Polar Regions and his nephew, Sir James Clark Ross (1800–62), discovered the North Magnetic Pole. Scotsmen, Dr John Rae (1813–93) and Thomas Simpson (1808–40), mapped out vast areas of the Arctic, and the first crossing was made by Sir Robert McClure, also a Scot.

Yet if these achievements are impressive, the Scots exploration of Africa changed the future of the continent. The religious zeal of the Lowland Scot made him the ideal African missionary. Hardy, dogged and determined to get a conversion, he bulldozed himself into the interior of Africa and opened it up.

James Bruce (1730–94), from Stirlingshire, explored Abyssinia and Sudan and discovered the source of the Blue Nile. His adventures were so extraordinary that it was years before anyone would believe what he had done. Bruce's reputation was not helped by having the sequel to *Baron Munchausen* dedicated to him.

Rev. John Campbell (1766–1840) discovered the source of the Limpopo River.

Mungo Park (1771–1806), who charted the Niger and mapped Nigeria, was born in Selkirkshire.

Hugh Clapperton (1788–1827) was the first white man to cross the Sahara and the discoverer of Lake Chad.

Alexander Laing (1793–1826) from Edinburgh discovered the source of the Rockell and was the first European to see Timbuktu.

David Livingstone (1813–73) from Blantyre was the most famous of all African explorers, and the man who discovered the Victoria Falls and the Zambezi River.

Scotsman James Grant (1827–92) discovered Lake Victoria and the source of the Nile, along with Englishman John Speake, and Lovett Cameron became the first man to cross equatorial Africa.

Joseph Thomson (1858–95) discovered Lake Rukwa and Thomson's Falls in Kenya.

And these were all natives of Scotland, or Scots of immediate descent. If one were to rope in all those of Scottish ancestry, the list of Scottish explorers expands enormously.

Including Neil Armstrong, the first man on the moon.

THE EMPEROR'S NEW KILT

He's a braw, braw Hielan' laddie, Private Jock McDade
There's not anither sodger like him in the Scotch Brigade
Rear'd among the heather, you can see he's Scottish built
By the wig, wig, wiggle, wiggle-waggle o' the kilt.
SIR HARRY LAUDER (1870–1950), SCOTS ENTERTAINER

The highlander and the kilt. The two go together like salt and pepper. Scotland has made this free-flowing garment famous all over the world – as well as proving that men *can* look tough in a skirt.

Problem is, the Scots didn't invent the kilt and, for most of their history, they didn't wear one.

The original Highland costume consisted of the *leine*, the *brat* and the *trews*. The *leine* was a large shirt, rather like a smock, and the *brat* was a circular cape-like mantle worn above it. The *trews* were coloured leggings – they could be worn long and over the feet, like tights, or short, like ancient cycling shorts.

Of these three, only the *trews* are still worn – usually in the armed forces – though now they look like trousers and are made of tartan. In fact, one might say, they *are* tartan trousers. Perhaps it's just too much, these days, to look menacing in tights.

The *brat* and *leine* were the common uniform in northern Scotland until close to the seventeenth century. The *leine* was very long and the bottom half was often pleated, making the lower part of the garment look somewhat like a skirt. This has been mistaken for the kilt, but is simply the lower part of the shirt.

In 1521, Scotsman John Major described highland dress in his *History of Greater Britain*.

> From the middle of the thigh to the foot they have no covering for the leg, clothing themselves in a mantle instead of an upper garment and a shirt dyed with saffron… The common people of the Highland Scots rush into battle having their body clothed with a linen garment manifoldly sewed and painted or daubed with pitch, with a covering of deerskin.

But around the end of the sixteenth century, a new variation of Highland dress began to develop – the belted plaid. This was neither a mantle nor a long shirt but a multipurpose garment that combined the best qualities of its two predecessors.

A chaplain visiting Scotland in 1689 described this new article of clothing.

> These pladds are about seven or eight yards long, differing in finess according to the abilities or fancy of the wearers. They cover the whole body with 'em from the neck to the knees, excepting the right arm, which they mostly keep at liberty. Many of 'em have nothing under these garments besides waistcoats and shirts, which descend no longer than the knees, and so they gird 'em about the middle . . .

For convenience, this long length of cloth was fastened in the middle by a belt. Up to 20 feet long and 5 feet wide, this plaid bore no resemblance to a kilt. The thickness, length and weight of the cloth protected the wearer from the treacherous Highland climate and could be used for all sorts of purposes – even as a bed.

Coloured with natural dyes, this large plaid or *Feileadh Mor* bore no resemblance to the Scottish national dress today. Nowadays, the image of the Scotsman is epitomised by the short pleated kilt – usually accompanied by an article of clothing that no highlander ever wore: a formally cut jacket.

But where did the 'little kilt' come from?

The idea of making the plaid shorter probably occured to several people, as a smattering of early pictures show. Yet, if any one man can lay claim to inventing and popularising the 'little kilt', ironically, it is Thomas Rawlinson, an English factory manager.

In the early eighteenth century, Rawlinson had a large number of highlanders working in his iron works at Lochaber, and all were still wearing their traditional long plaids. It was fairly obvious that a gigantic piece of cloth wrapped every which way was not the ideal uniform for working in a machine-based environment – especially one with lots of flames. Rawlinson, however, was very taken with the spirit of Highland garments and didn't want to make his workers abandon their traditional garb completely, so he devised a compromise. He simply took the bottom half of the belted plaid and isolated it, to form a garment of its own – the *Feileadh Beag* or 'little wrap', now known as the kilt.

Then, taken by the spirit of the whole enterprise, he went even further and had pre-pleated versions of this kilt made for himself and his business colleague MacDonald of Glengarry.

This new clothing innovation soon became all the rage and was so convenient that other highlanders started wearing it. When the Victorian craze for all things Scottish swept through the Lowlands and England, the kilt, not the trews or plaid, was adopted – despite its recent pedigree and questionable origin.

Today, people all over the world, Scots included, proudly wear their complex and frilly national dress to functions and parties. Jackets are velvet and ruffles and sparkly bits adorn this caricature of authentic Highland dress. Arguments rage over how the laces should be tied, how far down the jacket should come and what shape the buttons should be. It's hard to imagine highlanders arguing about *that* on the eve of battle.

The real Highland dress, the plaid, could be worn any way the wearer liked. It was invented to complement a life of hardship and rough living. It had no status. It was the very essence of functionality and simplicity.

Not surprisingly, these days it is virtually never seen.

DARK AND STORMY KNIGHTS

Non nobis Domine, non nobis sed Nomini Tuo da Gloriam.
(Not for us O Lord, not for us but in your name is the Glory.)
THE MOTTO OF THE ORDER OF THE KNIGHTS TEMPLAR

Few groups have created such a depth and breadth of legend as the Order of the Knights Templar – they have been accused of everything from having Satan's babies to being the guardians of the Holy Grail.

Yet, despite the name of the Knights Templar being recognised throughout the western world, few people know many details about the Order, their legends, or the effect they were to eventually have on the world.

And they certainly don't know the part that Scotland played.

Despite their mythological reputation, the Order of the Knights Templar had very practical origins – they were a European monastic military order formed around the beginning of the twelfth century to protect pilgrim routes to the Holy Land. During the early Crusades, they distinguished themselves as a formidable Christian fighting force

– and their merciless slaughter of the Muslim enemy was particularly appreciated by the Christians of the West.

As the Templar's reputation grew, however, so did their size and power. Within two centuries they had become a religious Frankenstein's monster, famed for the incredible wealth they amassed during the Crusades, rather than for their piety or skills in war – they are credited with the invention of banking in Europe. Though lending money was forbidden by the Church of Rome, the Templars were powerful enough to circumvent this, providing under-the-round-table financing for kings and major nobles on their campaigns.

It's a sad truth that power corrupts, and usually leads to violence. The Knights drifted from their original occupation as the defenders of Christianity and settled into the role of powerbrokers in armour. And that power was a threat to the established order in Europe – monarchies didn't like being in hock and the Papacy wasn't used to being defied. They began plotting to cut the Templars down to size.

People didn't do things by halves in the Middle Ages. In 1308 Philip of France arrested Jacques De Moilay, the Grand Master of the Knights Templar and four years later, a papal decree dissolved the Order entirely.

The assault on the Knights Templar was as swift and ruthless as any they had conducted against the Muslims. The Order was accused, en masse, of heresy and its members suddenly found themselves persecuted all across Europe. Their vast assets were then seized by the financially strapped Philip of France – which gives a clue to *his* reasons for wanting the Order out of the way.

Heresy was a pretty serious charge in fourteenth century Europe and, besides, nobody would support the Templars against the combined might of the Roman Catholic Church and the Kingdom of France. The hapless Knights found themselves without European allies and with no country willing to give them protection.

With one exception.

In Scotland, no order of suppression had been issued against the Templars, since, under Scots law, charges against the Order had been found not proven. This didn't mean much to the powers in Europe, who were determined to have the Templars stamped out. Any king seen to be giving the Knights shelter was liable to be excommunicated by Pope Clements, as well as incurring the wrath of Philip of France.

These deterrents, however, did not apply in Scotland. In the early fourteenth century, the king was Robert the Bruce – and he had already been excommunicated for killing John Comyn. Bruce also happened to be waging a campaign against Edward I of England, Philip's hated enemy. France was certainly not going to penalise such a valuable ally.

Shunned by the countries they had once protected, and with no chance of migrating east to non-Christian lands, many of the Knights Templar fled to Scotland.

Considering the recent events in their history, it wasn't surprising that the Order of the Knights Templar kept a low profile in their new home. Yet there is a distinct possibility that their arrival was one of the pivotal moments in Scotland's history

One of the famous stories of Robert the Bruce is the tale of his incredible victory over the English at the Battle of Bannockburn in 1314. The Scots and English armies had fought fiercely for hours, but Bruce's force was smaller and less well equipped – even though he held a superior position, he was by no means assured of victory.

The English were startled, however, to see a second Scottish army appearing over a nearby hill. Their nerve broke and the tide of battle turned in favour of the Scots. The second 'army' turned out to be a mass of local villagers coming to see if the battle had ended, so that they could scavenge among the bodies.

It's possible that this story is true, but there are some questionable aspects of the fable. It doesn't sound likely that a bunch of villagers – and quite a sizeable one at that – would show themselves so obviously to thousands of enemy soldiers waving swords. It's also rather hard to explain why a superbly trained English army who had fought all day against the legendary savagery of the Scots would run away upon spotting a bunch of unarmed women and children in rags.

The other version of the turn of battle is far less well known – that there really was a second army – the Order of the Knights Templar. According to legend, the Templars had agreed to accompany Bruce to Bannockburn, though they had no desire to fight against such overwhelming English forces. On realising that Bruce, despite all the odds, really did stand a chance of victory, they joined in on his side and won the day. Having helped the Scots to throw off the hated English oppression, the Templars were assured a safe haven and the gratitude of a victorious king.

There is no concrete proof that either version of the Battle of Bannockburn is true. What is known, however, is that Bruce gave the Knights Templar protection in Scotland after the Battle of Bannockburn, and insisted that his heart be taken on pilgrimage after he died.

Bruce was nothing if not a practical man. During his life, despite protestations of regret about murdering John Comyn, he had never actually bothered going on a pilgrimage. The decision to send his heart when he didn't need it any more sounds suspiciously like a mixture of Templar influence and Bruce pragmatism.

The famed secrecy surrounding the history of the Knights Templar is understandable given the persecution they had faced, but hinders the present-day untwining of fact and fable. But the Templar legend does crop up in Scotland at the most opportune moments.

Prince Henry Sinclair, for instance, is supposed to have had Templar assistance in organising his journey across the Atlantic. The reason for the support? The Templars were intrigued by the possibility of an escape route from Scotland, should they need it, and one that didn't go anywhere near the rest of Europe. Rosslyn Chapel, built by Sinclair's grandson, is almost a shrine to the Templars, and is reputed to have the Holy Grail buried underneath!

In the end, there was no need for a mass exodus. The Templars remained free from persecution in Scotland, although their glory days had well and truly gone. Never again would they approach the power they had held in the twelfth and thirteenth centuries. No longer any threat to the European powers, they found they could spread slowly back onto the continent.

There are tantalising hints that the Knights Templar in Scotland, however, retained some sense of their old influence. John Graham of Claverhouse (Bonnie Dundee) is said to have died at the Battle of Killiecrankie with the Grand Cross of the Templars round his neck and it is reported that Bonnie Prince Charlie gave a soirée in Holyrood Palace for the Order.

But the Knights Templar had an impact on the world in one department, not yet mentioned. In Scotland, they helped build and strengthen an organisation that is famous across the world today.

THE FREEMASONS

The origins of modern Freemasonry are said to have stemmed from the Order of the Knights Templar, who financed and escorted cathedral builders across Europe – and the two societies have always been inextricably linked in people's imaginations.

Freemasonry. It conjures up pictures of funny handshakes and men dancing around in moose antlers with their trousers rolled up. Yet the society of Freemasons has millions of members and inspires endless debates as to the exact extent of its considerable powers. Freemasons describe their philosophy as a 'universal brotherhood of men dedicated to serving God, family, fellow men and country' – and this brotherhood is the oldest, the largest, and certainly the most powerful fraternal order in the world.

Freemasonry is often viewed with deep suspicion. Though this may be due to the public's preference for gossip over asking questions, the Masons are still regarded as an insular and somewhat sinister organisation. It is no surprise, then, to find that the roots of modern Freemasonry are planted firmly in Scotland.

The Order of Freemasons stems from the craft of stonemasonry and has a history which stretches back as far as Ancient Egypt – as long as man has been building large stone structures, in fact. Modern Freemasonry, however, is derived from the organized guilds or unions of European stonemasons who constructed the cathedrals of the Middle Ages.

In the fifteenth century many craftsmen were fed up with the treatment they received from merchants and formed into associations, some growing so strong that laws were passed to restrict them. The Masons became the most powerful of these guilds – the skills of its craftsmen were in demand all over Europe. Unlike other classes of tradesmen, masons were allowed to travel freely from country to country, earning them the obvious title of 'Freemasons'.

The English and French have both laid claim to being the 'founders' of modern Freemasonry, but early masons in Scotland had the advantage of being encouraged and guided by the Knights Templar who had taken refuge there at the beginning of the fourteenth century. Under the Knights' protection, Freemasonry in Scotland flourished like nowhere else.

Unfortunately, Freemasons also managed to pick up the Templar's dubious reputation for secrecy – a legacy that persists to this day.

The oldest surviving Masonic minutes date from 1599 in Edinburgh and the oldest Masonic Lodge room still in use is at the Canongate Kilwinning Lodge No. 2. As early as 1491, Edinburgh authorities allowed their masons to 'get a recreation in the commoun luge'.

The Masonic 'Word' appears in Scotland around 1550 and there were 25 Scottish lodges operating before the eighteenth century, of which 20 survive to this day. There is no evidence of an English lodge before the eighteenth century.

In 1583 and 1598, Scotsman William Schaw was commissioned by King James VI with the task of re-organising the Masonic craft. He drew up the 'Schaw Statutes', which set out the duties of lodge members and imposed penalties for shoddy work. More importantly, he established the Masonic lodges as fixed permanent institutions, earning him the title 'the founding father of Freemasonry'.

Scotland was an ideal place for the Masonic Society to flourish – the Scots continued to use crude stone as a building tool after other nations had turned to carved bricks and early in the seventeenth century, when Masonic unions across Europe began to decline, Scotland is credited with upholding the craft.

But times change, and Freemasonry could not retain the power and respect it once held. To preserve their influence, the guilds began to admit men of prominence in society into their lodges – irrespective of whether they were craftsmen or not – setting up the system that exists to this day. This class of members became 'patrons' of the fraternity – known by the title 'accepted masons'.

At the conclusion of the seventeenth century, a radical transformation had evolved, with 'accepted masons' becoming predominant in the Order. As the actual craft of masonry faded into obscurity, the lodges of the Freemasons began to teach morals and philosophy rather than the art of hewing stone.

This new type of Masonic society, with its basic ideal that men are equal in moral worth rather than rank and station, was eminently well-suited to Scottish philosophy. In the class-conscious south, English lodges became the exclusive preserve of 'accepted masons' and tended to prohibit working men. In Scots lodges, however, noblemen and artisans could meet in lodges as brothers.

Freemasonry also appealed to the Scots' clannishness. In the northern hills, the highlanders had little use for masonry – they had clans of their own and had never shown much enthusiasm for cathedral building. But now Lowland Scots could band together too, in their Masonic groups, to indulge in their favourite pastimes: working hard, getting ahead in life – and keeping others out. The fact that the moral philosophy of Freemasonry was founded upon religious principles also suited the pious lowlanders.

It is no surprise, then, that Masonic philosophy had a great effect on the Scottish Enlightenment: that golden period when Scottish thought influenced the world. The three main Masonic principles of brotherly love, belief and truth, standing for the betterment of mankind, matched exactly the ideology of this period.

During the Enlightenment, Freemasonry was lauded as an organisation promoting egalitarian views, which would eventually be adopted by both the revolutionary American and French governments. A long line of eminent Scots were lodge members and the society actively encouraged up-and-coming talents like those of the poet Robert Burns.

Burns was a member of five different craft lodges and his famous line, 'a man's a man for a' that', perfectly sums up Masonic philosophy. He is a Masonic hero to this day – the St Thomas Scots lodge in Jamaica, for instance, refers to him as Bobby B and sets his poetry to Calypso tunes.

The eighteenth-century Masonic influence on the Scottish Enlightenment, and therefore on the western world, has now been forgotten, perhaps deliberately. Today, many people feel that Freemasonry has a strangely sinister aura, though they probably couldn't tell you why. Much of this suspicion comes from simple ignorance, and Masons are tainted by stigma ranging from the 700-year-old charges brought against the Knights Templar to the accusation that they were the original influence behind the Ku Klux Klan. (Scottish emigrants, certainly, were behind the Klan but there is no evidence that the Freemasons had anything to do with it.)

As for the Brotherhood's famed secrecy, well, the insular eighteenth and nineteenth century Scots wouldn't have had it any other way.

There are still debates today about just how influential the Order of Freemasons actually is. The truth is, nobody knows outside the society itself.

But it can certainly lay claim to some impressive members, including Buzz Aldrin, the astronaut; Louis Armstrong; J.C. Bach; Joseph Brant, chief of the Mohawks from 1743–1807; Robert Burns; Casanova; Winston Churchill; William Shakespeare; and Mozart.

THE TARTAN CURTAIN

Lord Aberdeen was quite touched when I told him I was so attached to the dear, dear Highlands and missed the fine hills so much. There is a great peculiarity about the Highlands and Highlanders; and they are such a chivalrous, fine, active people.

QUEEN VICTORIA, *OUR LIFE IN THE HIGHLANDS*

Scotland is generally viewed as one country, and today, of course, it is – though try telling someone from Glasgow they are related to an inhabitant of Edinburgh and you may get a different perspective. For the sake of expediency, Scotland is often described as an antagonistic mixture of different tribes who eventually settled into the entity known as the Scottish nation.

However, for most of Scotland's history the distinction between the 'Highlands' and the 'Lowlands' was an overriding one. 'Highland' and 'Lowland' are not entirely satisfactory definitions in themselves – the Lowland borders had virtual autonomy for a long period of time, whereas the northern and western Highlands and Islands were a Scandinavian power base for centuries. But to accurately chart the long, slow process of Scottish unification would be a book in itself – and a long one at that.

The polarity between Highlands and Lowlands is by far the most distinct of these Scottish divisions. Lowland history is easier to chart, being generally regarded as the 'civilised' section of Scotland – albeit one of the most warlike and contradictory civilisations of all time. The Highlands, however, remained an enigma long after most of the rest of Europe had been stuck with conventional labels. Its inhabitants were situated at the very corner of the continent, hidden behind a mountainous barrier, speaking a different language from the rest of Britain and totally resistant to integration with their Lowland and English neighbours.

Due to their own self-imposed isolation, no people have ever been so ripe for mythologising. Because of this, the highlander has undergone several radical makeovers without ever having a hand in these historical interpretations, simply going about the business of ignoring the rest of the world, apart from the occasional warlike foray into the south, blissfully unaware of having undergone transformation after transformation.

In fact, the notion of the Highlands as a separate national entity does not seem to have existed before 1300. Certainly there is no documentation of such a distinction in the plentiful records of the previous two centuries prior to 1300.

So where does the difference come from? How was this 'Tartan Curtain' formed?

The Scots chronicler, John of Fordun, was the first to describe the division of the two cultures:

> The manners and customs of the Scots vary with the diversity of their speech. For two languages are spoken amongst them, the Scottish and the Teutonic: the latter of which is the language of those who occupy the seaboard and plains, while the race of Scottish speech inhabits the highlands and outlying islands. The people of the coast are of domestic and civilized habits, trusty, patient and urbane, decent in their attire, affable and peaceful, devout in Divine worship yet always prone to resist a wrong at the hand of their enemies. The highlanders and people of the islands, on the other hand, are a savage and untamed nation, rude and independent, given to rapine, easy living, of a docile and warm disposition, comely in person but

unsightly in dress, hostile to the English people and language
and owing to diversity of speech, even to their own nation, and
exceedingly cruel.

No doubt which of the two *he* preferred.

To some extent, the reasons for the emerging division are obvious.
The Highland region was where Gaelic (called 'Scottish' by John of
Fordun) speaking and the geographic differences between northern and
southern Scotland made a handy physical dividing line. As time passed,
the idea developed that the Highlands were a far wilder place than the
Lowlands, socially as well as physically. Though the Lowlands were
never adverse to feuding, warring and general bloodshed, the
highlanders gradually gained a reputation for being far more excessive
in these departments.

This view was reinforced by cattle raids on the south and some truly
horrific clan feuds. In 1544, for instance, 400 members of the clan Fraser
engaged 700 members of Clan Ranald at the 'Battle of the Shirts'. They
fought from noon till dusk until, it was said, only 12 men were left alive.
Though this may be a slight exaggeration of the carnage, stories of this
ilk prompted the lowlanders to leave the highlanders well alone.
Resigning themselves to the occasional cattle raid, they viewed their
uncivilized northern neighbours with deep distrust and kept contact to
a minimum.

The highlanders were equally scornful of those in the south – they
raided them or traded with them, but they did not mingle with them.
The northerners cared nothing for national and world events – these
simply did not impact on their territory. Their isolated, tribal life was
more akin to the North American Indian than to the rest of Britain,
except that nobody, at that point, wanted their land.

By the eighteenth century, however, after successive Jacobite
uprisings, the Highlands posed a significant threat to the south – and
one that was perched on their very doorstep. At this point, the
highlanders underwent a major makeover. Now they were no longer
simply a violent nuisance: their attempts to put the deposed Stuart
dynasty back on the throne made them an actual enemy. There were
Jacobite sympathisers in the Lowlands and even in England, but not
enough to turn the tide of general opinion.

Dislike, in the south, turned to hatred. The highlanders were no
longer to be tolerated. Opinion had changed. They were vermin. They
were to be destroyed.

Southern writing and drama of the time gives a disturbing indication of this shift in perception. During and after the Jacobite rebellions the highlander was portrayed as a fool, rogue and beggar. It was good propaganda, minimising the panic of the Highland threat and helping to legitimise the destruction of the north and its way of life after the uprisings had been quelled.

The Jacobites' final defeat in 1746 was complete. Those who had supported Charles Edward Stuart were treated as traitors by the British government, even though the highlanders had never accepted the Hanoverian kings as their rulers. Those who had fought and those who had sheltered them were hunted down and slaughtered. The Gaelic language, the plaid, the bagpipes – every physical manifestation of Highland identity, were declared illegal. That many highlanders had actually supported the British government was of no consequence. They were penalised like all the rest.

The British government had set in motion a systematic deconstruction of the Highland way of life. Like the North American Indian, the highlander was publicly perceived as an ignorant savage, fighting a selfish battle against the 'progress' of a 'civilised' nation. Like the Indian, the disoriented and disillusioned highlanders were depersonalised to the extent that they could be treated as an inferior species. As such, they had lost the right to keep a way of life unchanged for hundreds of years. Their land was given away and the inhabitants replaced by sheep. Since there were no reservations onto which the government could herd these defeated savages, the highlanders found themselves, ironically, forced to relocate to America and Canada.

To be fair, the British government was not entirely to blame for this. They were quite happily aided by many Scottish lowlanders, who went along with the notion that their northern neighbours were pests rather than fellow countrymen. And to some extent, the highlanders' own leaders were responsible for the destruction of their people.

After Culloden, many of the old clan chiefs were dead, in hiding or utterly crushed and were succeeded by new chieftains, to whom the highlanders remained unreservedly loyal. But these new chiefs were no longer safe in their Highland strongholds. They owed their position, and their very survival, to the goodwill of the government in London.

Much as they might hate it, the chiefs had no real power and were well within the reach of British troops should they try to pretend they had. Many felt there was no longer any real point even remaining in the Highlands. The cold weather, austere life and clouds of midges were no longer offset by the feeling of actually being in charge of something. If they were going to be ruled by London, the clan leaders may as well go there and enjoy some of the benefits of civilization. After all, life in the south could be quite pleasant. The chiefs were not short of money – they were supported by rent and gifts from their loyal clansmen.

Comfort is seductive. Living in the south was a new experience for many of the chiefs and a very pleasant one at that. They soon slapped a veneer of sophistication onto their provincial manners, isolating them even further from the rough, uncomplicated highlanders left up north.

With each step, of course, the next became easier. Some of the clan chiefs, realizing they were never going back, proceeded to sell their land – land that offered far more monetary gain as a sheep farm or hunting ground than as an ancestral home. Those clan leaders who kept their lands found themselves victims of economic and social changes; they couldn't support the influx of relocated highlanders and good old-fashioned raiding was no longer an option. The highlanders were no better off under these sympathetic landowners than under the new owners from the south.

The mass exodus to other lands began.

By Victorian times great tracts of the Highlands had been cleared and the Jacobites were no longer a threat to the British nation, so now the northerners underwent yet another transformation. To the English, the tamed northern hills were far enough away to be exotic but close enough to be accessible; wild enough to be exciting but no longer life-threatening. As the threat of highlanders wreaking havoc on the rest of the country faded, the Barbarian in the North began mutating into the Noble Savage. Popularised in the romantic novels of Walter Scott and given the royal seal of approval by Queen Victoria, the Highlands were suddenly in vogue as a holiday destination. The highlander himself changed from the unpredictable bogeyman of the north to the stoic, silent guardian of their beauty. Tartan, once ridiculed and then banned, become a fashion statement.

Then, as the British Empire began its inexorable conquest of the globe, the highlander began his next transformation: Highland regiments began to form the backbone of the British army. For the first time, it was beneficial to the government if the highlander were seen as a natural warrior and heroic fighter. Highland loyalty to cause and clan, once feared, was now venerated, because that loyalty was to the British Empire. Now the highlander was Arnold Schwarznegger in a kilt, and had gone from being the historical equivalent of the *Terminator* to *Terminator II* – exactly the same character, but fighting for the good guys. In the nation's eyes he had gone from villain to hero without a change in expression.

There has been one last addition to the changing perception of the highlander. In the past, whether savage, rogue, beggar, fool or warrior, he has never exactly been Cary Grant. More oatcake than beefcake, the highlander was not famed for his sartorial elegance, charm or intellect. With exceptions like Walter Scott and R. L. Stevenson, Scots dramatists themselves haven't exactly helped, often portraying their race as a nation of dour but hardy workmen. With the coming of the age of cinema, British filmmakers made the highlanders into quaint anachronisms like *Geordie*, or the canny rural rustics of *Whisky Galore*. The Americans went to the other extreme and made *Brigadoon*, which seems as though it was written and filmed on another planet and *Bonnie Prince Charlie*, in which the eponymous hero looks like a girl.

But another shift has arrived. With the making of just three Hollywood blockbusters: *Highlander*, *Rob Roy* and *Braveheart*, the tartan-clad, kilt-wearing, northern Scot has become a sex symbol – a manly dynamo bristling with rough-hewn charm. The fact that none of the three leads were Scottish seems to have had no effect whatsoever on the popularity of this new myth.

The changing hand of history has made the despised highlander, not the lowlander, the hero of Scotland. Always a canny bunch, the Scots in the south have had no hesitation in jumping on this sexy Highland hero bandwagon, and the distinction between the Highlands and the Lowlands is fading once more.

Thanks to Hollywood, one day perhaps we will simply all be Scots.

THE STRIPE THAT GOES BOTH WAYS

The swindlers asked him to step a little closer so that he could admire the intricate patterns and marvellous colours of the material they were weaving. They both pointed to the empty loom, and the poor Prime Minister opened his eyes as wide as he could; but it didn't help, he still couldn't see anything.

'Tell us what you think of it,' demanded one of the swindlers.

'It is beautiful. It is very lovely,' mumbled the old Prime Minister, adjusting his glasses. 'What patterns! What colours! I shall tell the emperor that I am greatly pleased.'

HANS CHRISTIAN ANDERSEN, *THE EMPEROR'S NEW CLOTHES*

The Highlands were feared and despised by southern Scotland for hundreds of years but, by the 1850s, all that had changed. The highlanders were tamed and the land had become a trendy holiday destination. Highland dress, in a flamboyant style that real highlanders wouldn't even recognise, was well and truly in vogue. Ever since the fateful visit to Scotland by George IV in 1822 (see *Great Scott*), Britain had gone into a northern frenzy. Tartan, especially, was all the rage – to the extent that Queen Victoria designed her own, covering every wall, chair and servant in Balmoral Castle with the stuff.

The tartan bandwagon was suddenly full to overflowing. Two brothers, the Sobrieski-Stuarts, turned up from Poland claiming to be grandsons of Bonnie Prince Charlie. Naturally enough, they also just happened to be experts on the history of the tartan. In 1842 they produced a nattily titled book: *Vestiarrium Scoticum: from the Manuscript formerly in the Library of the Scots College at Douay; with an Introduction and Notes*. The book listed and illustrated 75 original clan tartans and was happily accepted by all and sundry as being authentic.

The Sobrieski-Stuarts were, in reality, John and Charles Allen. They were not related to Prince Charlie in any way, shape or form and knew no more about authentic tartans than the next con man. By the time this was realised, however, their bogus designs were firmly established in the cloth manufacturing industry and remain so to this day.

Nowadays, there seem to be more tartans in existence than there are Scots to wear them. Visitors to Edinburgh's tartan shops are pleasantly surprised to find that their surname, no matter how exotic it might be, is connected in some way to a Scottish clan. That this connection may be so far removed as to be preposterous is submerged by the desire to be entitled to some tartan or other. Sadly, even if the visitor really *is* related to a MacDuff or Sinclair, he will probably end up wearing a 'clan' tartan that no MacDuff or Sinclair ever designed or wore.

So are tartans just a worldwide confidence trick? Did the Scots ever really wear them? And if they did, how close a resemblance did *their* tartan bear to the complex multi-patterns that decorate all things Scottish today?

It is only recently that tartans came to be worn in the Lowlands in any shape or form. Tartan wearing in southern Scotland was sparked by Jacobite sympathisers in the eighteenth century, and was very limited. But a Victorian obsession with wearing anything perceived to be Scottish and stripy is largely to blame for tartan's emergence in southern Scotland. For most of the Lowland's history, the sight of a man wearing tartan would send the population running for the nearest weapon.

An Englishman named Fynes Morison, gave an excellent description of typical Lowland Scots in 1598 – and it is the very opposite from the normal chequered perception.

> The husbandmen in Scotland, the servants, and almost all in the country did wear coarse cloth at home, of grey or sky-colour, and flat caps, very broad. The merchants in cities were attired in English or French cloth, of pale colour or mingled black and blue. The gentlemen did wear English cloth, or silk . . .

Though he does go on to admit that:

> The inferior sort of citizens' wives and the women of the country did wear cloaks made of two or three colours of checkerwork – vulgarly called ploddan.

Hardly describes the complex tartans seen today, does it?

To search for the true origin of tartan we must look to the Highlands – the traditional bastion of the stripe that goes both ways.

It does seem a bit odd that such a fancy and complex pattern would become the trademark of a nation living a rough and immediate life in the inhospitable landscape of northern Scotland. If the lowlanders, who had access to some measure of civilisation, could only manage 'two or three colours of checkerwork', those scraping a living in the north were hardly likely to produce anything more fancy.

Highlanders lived in the rudest of houses, in crippling poverty, and had no use for anything ornate unless it was a weapon. This was a race bred for conflict – one that could up and move against a rival at a moment's notice. The idea that they would have spent their precious spare time weaving elaborately patterned garments to identify their family is far-fetched, to say the least. If you wanted to know which clan a particular highlander came from, you asked him. Their badge of identification was usually just that – a feather or some other symbol worn as part of their headgear.

Later romantic writers came up with an image of Highland tartan weaving that was impractical at best and often downright ridiculous. Their depictions conjure images of Highland womenfolk carefully plucking wool, spinning it by firelight and dying it with local plants to match an age-old pattern. This doesn't really come across as a realistic occupation for people whose main concern was the struggle to adequately clothe themselves. Highlanders had neither the time nor the inclination to make fashion statements.

The Highland 'big wheel', used for spinning, was rudimentary at best and didn't lend itself to the production of intricate weaves.

Instead, any cloth the highlanders wove was dyed using natural oils. It's fair to say that a range of clear bright colours was possible, but varying shades were pretty much out of the question and the delicate cross-stitching on the tartans seen today simply wasn't feasible.

Little is known of just how the highlanders did achieve their colours or what plant or fish oils they used as dye. In fact, remarkably little is known as to how the northern weavers might have achieved tartan – an odd state of affairs considering how massively popular it is today.

Martin Martin's 1703 publication *A Description of the Western Islands Of Scotland* gave a hint, now widely accepted, as to how some kind of complex tartan was possible in olden times.

> There is a great deal of Ingenuity requir'd in sorting the Colours, so as to be agreeable to the nicest Fancy. For this reason the Women are at great pains, first to give an exact Patern of the Plad upon a small rod, having the number of every Thread of the Stripe on it.

This would seem to indicate a fairly sophisticated, if painstaking, method of producing an identifiable woven pattern and was gratefully seized upon by later mass manufacturers as evidence that humble highlanders could produce the same complex patterns that they were now churning out. In fact, Martin's explanation was never backed up by any other chronicler and nobody is exactly sure what he meant – there are no other accounts of this mysterious weaving 'rod' in the Highlands. Nor were tartans woven by women, as Martin seems to indicate. Highland women had hard enough tasks in their day-to-day lives. Weaving wasn't one of them.

The Highland weaver was generally a skilled male individual who served a long apprenticeship. The Highland cloth, though harder and harsher than its southern counterpart, was well woven and the patterns brighter and more defined. But the cloth was dyed for contrast and there is no reason to believe it looked anything like the woven stripes we see today.

This doesn't mean that the history of the 'tartan' isn't fascinating – the earliest reports of native Scottish patterns go back almost two thousand years. Romans describe the ancient Celts as wearing bright colours and refer to their dress being 'striped' – though this could mean anything. Certainly, tartan is striped – but then so is a football scarf.

The earliest mention of the word 'tartan' comes from James V's treasurer in 1538:

> for iij elnes of Helande Tertane to be hoiss to the Kingis Grace . . .

This is often taken to be a reference to the famous Stuart tartan – tartan of the kings of Scotland. However, although the word used is definitely tartan, it gives no clue to what the cloth actually looked like. Royal Stuart tartan doesn't seem to have come into existence until the eighteenth century and was then hijacked and altered by George IV in the nineteenth century. The word tartan does not even necessarily have to refer to a chequered cloth. As late as the nineteenth century there are references to tartans that don't have anything to do with stripes. In 1825, for instance, a merchant ordered from Wilson's of Bannockburn 'plain green coloured tartan without pattern'.

A 1532 reference to tartan by George Buchanan seems to have more of a ring of truth:

> Their ancestors wore plaids of many different colours and numbers still retain this custom, but the majority now, in their dress prefer a dark brown, imitating nearly the leaves of heather, that when lying upon the heath in the day, they may not be discovered by the appearance of their clothes.

The idea that the highlanders' lifestyle might favour camouflaged dress rather than sticking out of the heather like sore thumbs seems a sensible one. And again, the fact that their ancestors were fond of bright colours doesn't necessarily refer to tartan. Lots of races wore bright colours. And though references to Highland dress become more numerous from this point, they again generally refer to 'diverse colours', which could mean any kind of combination or pattern.

Around this time, mentions of various clans distinguishing themselves by the colours and pattern of their dress begin to occur in literature. Again, this is a trait that can be ascribed to football teams, armies, or company employees, none of which wear tartan. In fact, from medieval times, the Scots had distinguished themselves mainly through heraldry. Family crests and coats of arms adorned castle walls, horses, shields and garments and were much more significant than any pattern on cloth.

In 1631, a German artist made a woodcut of Highland soldiers in the employ of Gustavus Adolphus, wearing what appear to be tartan outfits. This has been taken as the first visual evidence of ancient tartan wearing. The garments, however, have an almost quilted appearance that resembles some sort of sewn patchwork and look suspiciously like the type of quilted jerkin used as a medieval defence against arrows. And it must be remembered that these highlanders were fighting in Europe, not Scotland. They may have felt the need to identify themselves with a uniform they would not have needed in their native land.

In the 1570s, Bishop Lesley refers to garments 'seamed together with silk, commonly green or red'. This again gives the impression of some kind of sewn pattern, almost like quilting. But it still doesn't sound like tartan and, anyway, would only have been worn by the wealthy.

In 1618, the London poet John Taylor visited the Highlands and gave perhaps the most quoted account of early Highland dress. Finding himself part of a wealthy hunting party, he described them as wearing 'stockings made of a worsted stuff of divers colours, which they call Tartane'. Though the highlanders were obviously wearing something very distinctive, Taylor's description still seems rather unsatisfactory. Tartan is unique among patterns in that it is very easy to describe. Try describing paisley or tweed and see how far you get. Yet nobody up to this point has made the simple description 'dark cloth with coloured vertical and horizontal stripes' – a depiction of tartan which would be universally recognised today.

The obvious conclusion is that tartan simply didn't look like that then.

In fact, it is not until the eighteenth century that written depictions of tartan begin to even slightly resemble their modern versions. It is at this point that the first pictures appear showing highlanders in material that actually looks familiar.

Those pictures, however, reveal a disconcerting fact. Although the style of the tartan is similar to modern patterns, the tartans in those old pictures *are not the same as the tartans attributed to these clans today*. Not only that, but the tartans depicted in early paintings don't seem to suggest any uniformity *even among members of the same clan*.

It is entirely possible that these Highland dignitaries, aware that they were being captured for posterity, put on specially made ceremonial finery – outfits nobody wore in ordinary life.

Highland testimonies, recorded during the eighteenth century Jacobite rebellions, reveal a startling fact. Highlanders themselves admitted that they identified friends and enemies by the emblems they wore in their bonnets, *not* by any tartans they wore.

But how could some Victorian tartan myth so completely replace historical reality? The answer lies in an 80-year gap which allowed the tartan to disappear and be 'rediscovered'. The Jacobite rebellions posed such a threat to the order of the day that the British government banned all things associated with Highland identity – including their dress. This was not an unusual move – a defeated army is never allowed to go around wearing its uniform. The highlanders, however, fought in the same outfit they wore the rest of the time and so the bewildered northerners found their everyday dress was banned entirely.

In the end, the ban was lifted to allow highlanders in the British Army a unique uniform – one that would make them feel they were still part of a warrior tribe. Having proved themselves valuable assets in military campaigns, the powers that be rewarded the northerners by allowing the 'reintroduction' of their national dress. But this new 'tartan' was designed to be a uniform – and each soldier's tartan *had* to look the same.

These identical tartans were no longer produced in the tiny communities of the Highlands – instead, the patterns were mass-manufactured elsewhere. It is somewhat ironic that the only other recipients of mass-produced tartans were the slaves in the USA, since the new tartan was cheap, durable and easily identifiable.

The 80-year gap had given cloth manufacturers the perfect excuse to produce in bulk whatever patterns they liked. This may well have come as something of a shock to the many highlanders who had largely ignored the ban – a defiance they could easily get away with, as *their* tartans were diverse and unidentifiable.

The ban allowed tartan mythology to weave itself inextricably into historical reality and the result was a new type of cloth entirely – colourful, durable, and largely artificial.

It is only at this point that the first books of complex and identifiable tartans begin to appear – there would have been nothing to describe before. Many, like those of the Sobrieski-Stuarts, are complete fabrications (excuse the pun). Others, like the lavishly illustrated *The Costumes of the Clans* published by R. McIan in 1845, run the gamut from the possible to the unbelievable.

By this time, the Victorians were clamouring to find any vague Scottish lineage allowing them to wear Highland dress. If one wasn't forthcoming, they were quite willing to make it up. The possibility that highlanders didn't wear tartans to distinguish their clans, and that anyone was entitled to wear any pattern they wanted, was roundly ignored. The Victorian era's equal passion for etiquette led to the ridiculous situation of books distinguishing between general tartans, hunting tartans, dress tartans and even funeral tartans – dress codes that the real clansmen would never have even considered.

Serious attempts were finally made to accurately record tartan with the 1850 publications of *Authenticated Tartans of the Clans and Families of Scotland* and *The Clans of the Highlands of Scotland*. But by now, the distinction between what was real and what was not had blurred beyond recognition and even the most scrupulous researcher was floundering in misinformation. The very people who should have been able to shed light on the whole affair, the clan chiefs, seemed to have less idea than anyone what their tartans were supposed to look like.

There are some who think this may be because the chiefs were angling for nicer tartans. A more logical explanation was that they simply didn't know.

From the day in August 1822 when George IV arrived to visit Edinburgh, Scotland has officially been the tartan race. What started as a fashion craze to welcome a fat monarch on a state visit has become an overwhelming part of the Scots national identity.

The fact that today's tartans are not authentic in pattern, colour, fabric or method of production has been conveniently swept under a national tartan rug.

SCOTS AWAY

Lord, grant that I may always be right, for Thou knowest I am hard to turn.
SCOTS–IRISH PRAYER

Scots have a rather enviable reputation. They are known, despite an affinity for hard drink, for their friendliness, enthusiasm and good humour. Scots have sexy accents. Scots are likeable.

It seems logical that the Scot got this happy reputation through a history of good conduct on other continents. After all, enough Scotsmen ended up on far-flung shores – a deadly mixture of land clearances and abject poverty in their home country saw to that. And the Scots flourished in many of the places where they settled. They were pious and well educated and brought those virtues with them: small wonder they are well liked around the world.

Easy to assume, but not necessarily true. As recently as the 1970s, the Scottish football fan was hated as the archetypal drunken hooligan abroad – a role that, thankfully, has been taken over by the species' English counterpart.

Throughout history, the Scots have flourished in other countries.

However, this doesn't mean that anyone there could stand them.

And sometimes it is easy to see why.

The Scots made their first serious forays abroad in medieval times – and rather successfully too. In the Middle Ages, Germanic lands were so filled with well-to-do Scottish peddlers that the word *Schotte* meant 'peddler' as early as 1330.

The Scots brought over their own women to marry and kept their own schools, charities, churches, hospitals and language. Their hard work ensured quick success, but they remained clannish and resolutely insular, contributing little to the culture of the existing population. This aloofness, isolation and suspicion of all things non-Scottish eventually became a despised trademark in every country they settled.

In Germany, the Scots aroused so much hostility that they faced brutal discriminatory laws, violence and imprisonment and by the end of the seventeenth century, the gates of many towns were shut against them. A threat to naughty children in Prussia was *Warte bis der Schotte kommt* – 'look out, the Scot will get you'.

It took years of stubborn resistance before emigrant Scots finally succumbed and integrated into the Germanic nations. One of the signs, perhaps, of their newfound Germanic pride was the raising of a petition to ban any more Scottish peddlers.

This pattern was repeated in other European countries. Even traditional Caledonian allies like the medieval French coined a proverb *Fier comme un Ecossais* – 'touchy as a Scot'. In Denmark, the *Skotters* got rich and infuriated the town merchants by peddling directly to the people. It wasn't long before they became scapegoats whenever the Danish government thought it expedient. In 1578, the inhabitants of Lund were actively warned off dealing with 'Netherlanders and Scots'.

In Sweden, the magistrates of Stockholm complained that the Scots 'did oust all native competition. All the best trade they draw to themselves.' Scots settled as far east as Russia, though these lands were so vast that the Scots' success was never threatening. Even so, native Russians described the incomers, progress as 'irksome'.

Medieval Poland, a country with very little commercial experience, became a Mecca for enterprising Scotsmen, who faced virtually no competition from the natives. Forming their own impregnable units, they worked their way up from peddlers to shopkeepers to bankers. Scottish success in Poland was so great that it caused consternation back in England – where the union of Scots and English crowns was being brokered. One dissenter voiced his objection by saying 'if we admit them into our liberties we shall be overrun with them . . . witness the multiplicities of the Scots in Polonia.' He had a point. By the seventeenth century Poland held over 30,000 prosperous Scots.

The story of the Polish Scots followed a familiar pattern. The immigrants' insularity and clannishness led to a native backlash and, in 1594, King Sigismund III issued a mandate against 'Jews, Scots and other vagabonds'.

There have been many comparisons made between the Scots and the Jews abroad. Sir Reginald Coupland declared 'It is at least a curious thing . . . that the races which wander the widest, Jews and Scotch, should be the most clannish in the world'. The Scots/Jewish politician, Manny Shinwell, took the association even further:

> There is a link between the Scots and the Jews. In fact I'm not sure myself that Scotland isn't the twelfth tribe of Israel. We always lost a tribe somehow or other. Why? It was on the rampage – off on its own – independent, constructive, destructive; it must have been the Scots tribe.

Despite these similarities, the Scots fared much better in other countries than their Jewish counterparts. When the British Empire swept the globe, Scotsmen who resided in other countries found themselves part of that powerful movement by virtue of their origins. They could leave and explore the possibilities of new-found global power or remain where they were and bask in their elevated status. The Jews had no such luck.

With the exception of the Jewish race, the Scots in various European countries held on to their own identity longer than any other immigrants. Unlike the Jews, however, the Scots eventually gave in, becoming part and parcel of their adopted nation. Even in Poland, Scotsmen finally gave up their cherished language and culture – even their names. MacLeod, for instance, became Machlajd and Weir became Wajer.

This leads to a rather intriguing possibility. In the 1980s Lech Walesa became a hero by uniting Poland against the oppression of the mighty USSR. The trade union leader was quoted as saying his ancestors arrived in Poland from 'somewhere in Western Europe'. Looking at the name it is perfectly possible, as well as extremely appropriate, that Walesa is actually descended from the clan Wallace.

Closer to home, the story was no better. In England the Scots had acquired a well-earned reputation as the neighbours from hell: Scottish attempts to set up a colony in the south were usually hampered by a tendency to burn out the original inhabitants. However, the Union of Crowns then the Union of Parliaments brought the two nations inexorably closer and more and more Scots found themselves drawn to the South, this time settling rather than raiding.

The Scot may have been a welcome addition to the English army, but having one living in the next house was a different matter. Anti-Scottish sentiment crept into all strata of English life. The politician John Wilkes summed up the suspicions of many:

> Into our places, states, beds they creep
> They've sense to get what we want sense to keep.

English insecurity was demonstrated by the Scots being viewed as sexual aggressors – a parallel to the uneasy insults Southern American whites directed at blacks. There was even a claim that the Scottish minister Lord Bute was sleeping with King George III's mother. By the late eighteenth century, Scotsmen were being parodied on the English stage and in the press as avaricious, power hungry and determined to take the best jobs in the country.

English fears were not without foundation. Faced with opportunities they'd never had up north, the Scots once again set about acquiring money and power with a vengeance, until they had a very noticeable influence in England. As the historian Christopher Smout put it, the Scots were beginning to exert a 'pull on the core, the tail beginning ever so slightly to wag the dog'. The Scottish 'takeover' is reflected in the anecdote about a Lowland businessman's return from his first trip to London.

'How did you find the English?' asked his curious neighbours.

'I canna rightly say,' replied the traveller. 'I only dealt with the heids o' departments.'

In England it was more difficult for the Scot to keep to himself – he was, after all, British as well as Scottish. Acquiring English customs and manners wasn't so bad for a Scot who could easily nip back to his own country and be as nationalistic as he pleased. The Scots, after all, had no real adversity to being British – it was becoming a pretty impressive Empire after all – they just didn't want to be English.

This British identity came to be adopted not only by Scots in England, but also those in Lowland Scotland. The consequences were obvious. The population of England was five times that of Scotland – what was considered 'British' was dominated by sheer southern numbers.

Unfortunately, size does matter. Eventually England referred to Scotland simply as 'North Britain'.

Oddly enough, it was in Ireland that Scots had the most intrusive and destructive effect – rather ironic since many of them came from Ireland in the first place. Though the Scots could spread through the infrastructure of other countries like a virus, it has been pointed out that they never started a successful colony of their own. Their one big attempt, the Darien colony in Panama, failed so miserably that it crippled Scotland financially and pushed them into a union with England.

What is forgotten, and with good reason, is that the Scots did put together one immensely successful colony – in Northern Ireland.

Successful for the Scots that is.

At the turn of the seventeenth century, James VI of Britain was facing all sorts of problems, both from unruly Scots and unruly Irishmen. With typical disregard for his own subjects, he came up with a cruel but simple solution. Get them to fight each other. Between 1605 and 1620 James 'relocated' around 20,000 Lowland Scots to Ireland.

The Scots were fervent Presbyterians. The Irish were Catholics.

Unlike the Highland/Lowland division of Scotland, there was no physical boundary between the two sides and not even the vaguest sense of national unity.

The Scots walked all over the Irish. As Professor Dewar Gibb pointed out, the Scots 'believed they were of a superior race and they meant to keep that race pure'. They quickly assumed power and established military and economic power bases through the country. This was something the British monarch did not expect and certainly did not want. Now the Scots held the reins of power in Ireland and could start considering how to take revenge on the people who had dumped them there in the first place.

The English government moved quickly to redress the situation, imposing so many taxes and import controls on the exiled Scots that their newly acquired power and wealth were destroyed. The Presbyterians had been forcibly uprooted from the mainland and they certainly weren't going back there. In desperation, they looked around for somewhere else to settle. And America beckoned.

During the seventeenth century, when the American colonies were being developed, a comparatively small number of Scots had emigrated to the New World. The dreaded 'Highland Clearances' were far off and most of the Scottish population had no intention of living anywhere but Scotland.

Perhaps it was just as well. The Scots who had arrived in the New World were just as unpopular there as they were everywhere else. Once again, their superior attitude and antisocial behaviour made them unwelcome. The Dutch government of New York passed a law restricting the activities of Scottish traders and in the English colonies, Scots were actually prohibited from holding office.

By the eighteenth century, the eastern seaboard of North America had been settled and was becoming quite a comfortable place to live. The soil was fertile, trade was good and the original natives had either been massacred or driven off. The settlers, predominantly German and English, seemed quite happy where they were.

Yet there was an entire continent to the west, a wilderness waiting to be opened up. There was no telling what riches it might hold – if anybody could get up the energy to exploit it.

Then the colonial planners had a brainwave – they turned their attention to the Scots in Ireland. They weren't considered as bright as the colonial settlers already there, but they were hardy and adaptable. As one colonist succinctly put it, the Scots in Ireland were 'perhaps the most disposable people in all of Christendom'.

Recruiting agents from the colonies were dispatched across the Atlantic and found a population of desperate Scots living in poverty in Ireland. With a little effort, and a lot of lying about how friendly America was, they persuaded the Scots to emigrate *en masse*. These agents may have promised an easy life in the New World, but that wasn't what awaited the immigrants. The colonists who were already there considered the eastern seaboard to be full. If the Scots wanted to settle they'd have to go further west.

This, of course, was the plan. The Scots would form an excellent line of defence between civilisation in the east and the Indian hordes in the west. Sneaky, but undeniably effective. Unfortunately the colonists' scheme depended on the Scots being suitably grateful for being rescued from poverty. The Scots were not. They settled down on the east coast along with everyone else and refused to budge.

To the horror of the existing inhabitants, the Scotch-Irish (as the Americans called them) were joined by more and more immigrants from Scotland itself. Once again these Scots built up their own insular communities – developing at a pace that engendered fear and resentment in equal measures. According to Andrew Hook in his book *Scots and America*, the Scots were 'certainly the most unpopular national group in the colonies'.

In Virginia, for instance, the English had a flourishing tobacco trade when the Scots began arriving in the early eighteenth century. These new immigrants were furious workers and, more importantly, were willing to seize any new opportunity that might make them a few dollars. As well as tobacco, they began to trade Virginia wood, iron, cotton and tar. They tracked across inhospitable mountains and opened stores so they could deal directly with isolated farmers. They were the first to trade by giving credit – this wasn't a great leap for clansmen used to dealing on trust (and capable of delivering retribution if that trust was betrayed).

Other settlers simply couldn't compete. Scots gained control of so much of Virginia's commerce that, between 1750 and 1775, Glasgow's share of the British tobacco industry rose meteorically from 10 per cent to 52 per cent.

Naturally, as the Scots drove the other Virginian settlers from the tobacco trade, resentment against them increased in every strata of the state's community. The great writer Daniel Defoe expressed his concern that Scots were taking over the place while common mobs ransacked Scottish houses and 'redistributed' the wealth inside.

As the War of Independence neared, feelings ran even higher. American plays such as *The Patriots* and *The Fall of British Tyranny* presented the Scots as stupid, greedy and immoral. Their stubborn refusal to mix with the local population made them far easier to isolate as a group. Their financial success, however, meant power and many colonial governors had risen from their ranks – governors who now administered the hated policies of George III of Britain with the same unflinching efficiency that had made them successful in the first place. When the first draft of the *Declaration of Independence* was written, Scotsman John Witherspoon had to insist that they take out a phrase complaining that King George had sent 'not only soldiers of our common blood, but Scotch and foreign mercenaries'.

In 1782 the Georgia House of Assembly even banned Scots from settling in Georgia. When they were finally allowed in, they were as pushy and arrogant as ever and immediately began to take things over. The Scots-Irish in Georgia used the phrase 'crackers' to describe themselves – a word still used in Scotland and Georgia to describe someone of worth. However, this is a recent innovation. Though the Scots-Irish were always proud of the moniker, the early Georgians used it as an ethnic slur.

In New York State the Scots went too far. During the War of Independence, highlanders joined forces with the Indians and conducted a terrorist campaign against the revolutionary families, to the extent of butchering women and children. When the war ended they were the only group forced to leave the newly formed states. They trekked northwards and settled in Canada.

Through all of this unpopularity, Scots doggedly kept making money. Having come from a land where the soil was poor, life was brutal and you fought frequently for what was yours, the Caledonian immigrants were not going to back down to anyone. Despite massive prejudices against them – and partly because of them – they persisted in their clannish ways, trusting nobody but their own kind and resolutely building up their wealth.

When the eastern seaboard really did become too small and over-developed for their tastes, the Scots finally headed west. They had never been afraid of tackling the wilderness – they just hadn't seen the point until they'd taken as much of the colonists' land and trade as possible.

The Scots and Scots-Irish were perfect for taking on the new frontier. In *Westering Man*, historian Bill Gilbert surmised that their flaws became strengths when it came to tackling the wilderness.

> They were not overburdened with abstract principles or
> conventional ethics, but they were mortally stubborn about
> expressing their interests . . . They had become a very hard or,
> as some of their critics claimed, even a brutal people. But the
> North American frontier was a hard brutal place.

The brutal Scots-Irish attitude was one that had to be adopted by the masses that came west after them, no matter what their nationality. In the wilderness, to be weak or compassionate was to die.

Farther south, the Presbyterian pioneers from mainland Scotland headed for the Great Plains. They were hardy, self-reliant and oblivious to danger. Tough and unbending, they placed great importance on religion and education and founded churches and schools wherever they went.

Even further south, the highlanders were pushing westward from their colonies in North Carolina. They had the distinct pioneering advantage of being liked by the Indians. Both peoples lived simple tribal existences, had been thrown off their ancestral lands and wore feathered headgear for identification – many Native Americans thought of them as brothers. It is another feather in the highlanders' caps that they reciprocated this sentiment. The Native American experienced more genuine warmth and honesty from the highlanders than from any other group who landed in North or South America – quite a feat considering the highlanders went to great lengths not to mix with anyone else.

And this, in the end, is the truly black legacy of the Scots abroad. Their unflinching policy of superiority and non-integration manifested itself in ways which are viewed with horror today. To the Scots are attributed the introduction of the lynch law in 1763. Scots-Irish also started the Ku Klux Klan in Pulaski, Tennessee – using Robert the Bruce's immortal *Declaration of Arbroath* as the basis for their philosophy. At first the Klan (a variation, of course, on clan) were only concerned with keeping their colonies 'pure' of outsiders. These 'outsiders' were not just the black population – it was anyone who wasn't Scots-Irish.

But the Scots have always taken things to extremes and the Klan's fundamental philosophy was only one step away from outright racism – as the world now knows to its cost. The burning cross, forever associated with the oppression of American blacks, was originally the method used to summon highlanders to fight.

The first supposedly scientific work on race in modern times was *The Races of Men* published by Edinburgh anatomist Robert Knox in 1850. In it he put whites at the top and blacks at the bottom of the racial hierarchy.

In North Carolina in 1905, a Scots minister called Thomas Dixon Junior wrote a novel called *The Clansman*, in which the Ku Klux Klan are rapturously described as 'the reincarnated souls of the Clansmen of Old Scotland'. The book was the basis for D.W. Griffith's epic movie *Birth of a Nation*.

Americans today treat the clannish and self-important aspects of Scots as a joke – a perfect example is the Scottish shopkeeper in the TV comedy show *Saturday Night Live*. His catchphrase, 'If it's not Scottish it's crap', perfectly captures the notion of Scots superiority and plays it for laughs.

How quickly people forget.

WHERE CREDIT IS DUE

This celebrated Scot
This schemer without equal
Who by the rules of Algebra
Has put France in the Hospital
EIGHTEENTH—CENTURY FRENCH POEM

Scots have had an important influence on the financial world. There are some who would say that this is to be expected from a nation famed for being tight-fisted penny-pinchers, who would sell their own grandmother. Be that as it may, Scotland is responsible for the watermark, the investment trust, the industrial bank, the first savings bank and the overdraft – the debt of generations of students rests on Scottish shoulders.

Scots were also behind the principle of banks holding notes for each other, large-scale joint-stock banking and motor insurance. They founded the Canadian banking system, the US Bank and the Bank of England – though, to be fair, an Englishman founded the Bank of Scotland.

Although its origins go back to ancient times, modern accounting was also largely developed in Scotland. In the mid-seventeenth century, George Watson in Edinburgh was the first full-time accountant in Western Europe and Alexander Heriot began teaching bookkeeping in the city around the end of the seventeenth century.

Stirring stuff indeed.

To be honest, banking isn't really an area where Scotland leaps to acknowledge its influence – 'the cradle of accounting' just doesn't have the right romantic ring – and as a national image it certainly isn't in the same league as that of a kilt-wearing Highlander running across the heather, waving a sword. Yet the Scots should revel in that dichotomy: they were the kind of people who would keep a careful account of what they'd taken from you at knifepoint.

One Scot showed that there was indeed a romantic side to matters financial. A gambler, womaniser and convicted killer, he was the first to spread the idea of producing paper money and giving credit across Europe. And, in doing so, he changed the course of western civilization.

His name was John Law.

In 1695 the *London Gazette* ran a short article about him.

> Captiane John Lawe, a Scotchman, lately a Prisoner in the King's-Bench for murther, aged 26, a very tall black, lean Man, well shaped above Six foot high, large Pockholes in his Face, big high-Nosed, speaks broad and low, made his escape from the said Prison. Whoever secures him so he may be delivered at the said Prison, shall have £50 paid immediately by the Marshal of the King's-Bench.

John Law (1691–1729) obviously had a few friends in high places, for this description does not fit him at all. He was handsome and soft spoken and had a reputation as a ladies' man. 'Beau' Law was being held in prison for the killing of another man in a duel: his reprieve was held up by the legal machinations of the dead man's brother. Law decided not to wait and see which way the scales of justice tipped. Instead, he made his escape and fled to the continent, and exercising admirable caution, he didn't return to London for 26 years.

Not a great deal is known about Law's adventures over the next 10 years, but stories of his wild escapades filtered back to his friends in Scotland and England. He moved first to Amsterdam, where he studied the principles of banking. Next, he appeared in Paris, where he persuaded a lady to leave her husband and elope with him to Italy. In Italy, he maintained an affluent lifestyle for himself and his mistress courtesy of the gambling tables of Venice and Genoa – where his skill was so uncanny that many believed he had figured out a system to beat the odds.

Around 1705, he popped up in Scotland touting the radical idea of using paper money and credit rather than traditional coinage. This concept aroused quite a bit of interest, but Law's timing couldn't have been worse. The Scottish parliament was about to be united with its English neighbour and as soon as this happened, Law was no longer safe from the English judicial system. He took off for the European mainland while he still had his liberty.

Law had decided he was onto a financial winner, however, and persisted in his efforts to implement paper money. In France, he tried to convince the ministers of Louis XIV that his ideas made monetary sense, but was again thwarted by circumstance. Law was a Protestant and, in the eyes of the Catholic Louis XIV, that made him little more than a heretic. The adventurer wisely took himself elsewhere, in case he found himself an unwilling guest in the Bastille.

There is no doubt that Law had a magic touch with money – equalled only by his ability to be in the wrong place at the wrong time. Back in Italy, he was so successful at gambling that both the Genoese and Venetian authorities 'suggested' he relocate to another city. He moved to Turin, tried Holland again, and then returned to Paris, still trying to get some financial institution to take his proposals seriously.

For once, Law arrived at a fortuitous moment. In 1715 Louis XIV died and France was taken over by the Duke of Orleans, ruling as regent for the infant Louis XV. The Duke of Orleans was more open-minded than the despotic Louis XIV and was willing to listen to Law's audacious proposals.

He liked what he heard.

In 1716, Law was give permission to set up the *Banque Générale* a private joint-stock bank that could issue banknotes. This was a new concept in European finance. Law's dream had come true: now he virtually had a licence to print money.

The bank became an unqualified success, so much so that the regent converted it into a state institution. Law was becoming an unstoppable force. He envisioned the 'Mississippi Scheme': a grand project to colonise the vast tracts of land that are now Louisiana. Law's company was fundamental to the strong French influence in the state today and he is directly responsible for the founding of New Orleans.

To implement his vision, Law formed the Mississippi Trading Company, a corporate giant which absorbed almost every other trading company in France, and then embarked on more and more ambitious projects – including the liquidation of the country's national debt. The great Scots economist, Adam Smith, wrote later that Law's system was 'the most extravagant project both of banking and stock-jobbing that perhaps the world ever saw'.

Shares in the Mississippi Trading Company went through the roof.

Aware that he was onto a good thing, Law, with typical Scottish shrewdness, converted to Catholicism in 1718 and became a French citizen. With the barriers of foreign nationality and religion removed, his star rose ever higher. He was elected a member of the *Académie Français*, and in 1820 was appointed Controller-General of the nation's finances. After the Duke of Orleans, he was now the most powerful man in the country.

In England, Law unsurprisingly received a pardon for his crime and he was also given the freedom of the city in his native Edinburgh.

But Law had that fatal Scots flaw: the tendency to go just a bit too far. His ambition had exceeded even his considerable ability. Stretched to breaking point in their attempts to fund his vast schemes, Law's financial institutions printed too many banknotes and, to compensate, French prices soared to ridiculous heights.

When the crash came it was catastrophic. On 21 May 1720, Law reluctantly agreed to a devaluation of both paper money and company shares. The Mississippi Trading Company's stock plummeted, thousands of investors lost everything they had and there was a stampede to try and convert paper money back into coinage. Inflation ran riot and the financial institutions were plunged into chaos.

In one fell swoop, the economy of France was ruined.

Law knew from experience when he had outstayed his welcome, and figured that this time he'd be lucky to get away with his life. In the panic, he slipped quietly out of France and back to England.

The disgraced financial wizard still had a plethora of ambitious ideas, but now nobody would take a chance on any of his grand schemes. He could not even raise the capital to win back a fortune at his forte – gambling. Like France, he was broke.

He died in 1729, destitute and forgotten, in a Venetian lodging house.

Though it was too late to be of any consolation to him, Law was still remembered by the French – they hated him with a passion. The French foreign minister even sent an ambassador to Venice to gain possession of Law's papers. He hoped to find one last system that would allow him to recoup some losses: the secret to Law's uncanny success on the gambling tables. If Law did have a method of cheating these early casinos, however, he took it to his grave.

It is a great shame that no government ever gave John Law a second chance. He may have gone to excesses, but his ideas were fundamentally sound and his monetary policies were eventually adopted all over Europe. The banknotes in your pocket today are there because of John Law.

You win some and lose some, but Law knew the secret of making finance romantic.

You have to be willing to take a gamble.

John Law had a Scots contemporary who made an even greater impression on world finance than he did, though his life wasn't nearly so romantic.

Adam Smith was the economist who provided the ideological fuel for the Industrial Revolution, a conflagration that swept away a centuries-old order. He quite literally changed the structure of civilisation.

Smith's fundamental idea was that 'a democratic society, driven by the self-interest of its people competing against one another, can generate more wealth than the same society, ruled by a government that tries to regulate the minute details of economic life'.

His book, the masterpiece *Wealth of Nations*, is still the gospel of economists and even former hard-line communist countries like Russia and China are beginning to adopt his economic policies.

Like or loathe his brand of philosophy, Adam Smith introduced capitalism to the world.

PRINCE CHARMING

If Prince Charles Edward Stuart had won at Culloden 250 years ago this month there would be precious few songs about him. We might not have gone so far as to put the Butcher of Cumberland on shortbread tins, but Bonnie Prince Charlie, in the Scottish psyche, would have been irredeemably diminished by success.

MICHAEL FORSYTH, SECRETARY OF STATE FOR SCOTLAND

In all of Scotland's history, one event still has more power to arouse Scots passion than any other – the doomed Jacobite uprising of 1745. Bruce and Wallace are heroes from a dim and distant past but the repercussions of the '45 can still be seen in the empty Highlands today. Since many Scots think one decent warrior beats a plethora of great thinkers, the leader of the country's last military foray – Charles Edward Stuart – has become one of the country's most prevalent icons.

The admiration Scots feel for Bonnie Prince Charlie, the 'King over the Water', is encapsulated in the poem by Lady Nairn:

> Bonnie Charlie's now awa
> Safely owre the friendly main
> Many a heart will break in twa
> Should he ne'er come back again
> Will ye no come back again?
> Will ye no come back again?
> Better loved you canna be
> Will ye no come back again?

But what makes Charles Stuart such a powerful figure in Scottish mythology? Was he really a god among men, or is there another reason for the tartan pedestal he is likely to occupy for all time?

In 1688 the last of the Stuart kings, James VII of Britain, was deposed by the Hanoverian dynasty. The Stuarts had ruled Scotland, then (from 1603) Britain, since 1371. James was an unpopular king. The Scots had tended to stick by their monarchs, no matter what their faults, but England was a different matter. The English had already executed one Stuart king because of his authoritarian approach to the government. They were not about to put up with the high-handedness of another. When the replacement monarch, William of Orange, landed at Torbay, James stood every chance of repulsing the threat to his throne. Yet his leadership skills deserted him when he needed them most. Rather than fight, he effectively abandoned his superior army and fled to permanent exile in France.

The deposed Stuart line still had scattered support throughout Britain but their stronghold was the Scottish Highlands. While Britain had become mostly Protestant, the Highlands had remained, like the Stuarts, Catholic and were loyal to the man they considered their rightful king. It may well be that more of Britain than it seemed shared this sentiment. The difference was that the highlanders were prepared to act on this belief. They were men of action, not words.

The northern clans immediately set about trying to return James VII to the throne, resulting in the Highland war of 1689–91. It was a failed attempt and the uprising of 1708 fared no better – not all the highlanders were willing to fight for a king who lived in London and had consistently ignored them. In reality, the Jacobites who did rise stood little chance against trained government troops who were better armed, better disciplined and far more numerous. Only the highlanders' legendary ferocity gave James even a sporting chance.

Undeterred, the hard-core Jacobite supporters rose again in 1715 to support James VII's son, also called James. They were no more successful.

After this the British government, determined to make sure that there were no more rebellions, built a system of roads and forts that linked the strategic points of northern Scotland. Further unrest would be much easier to quell.

In time, both James VII and his son became used to exile and it looked as though they were never coming back. The government army grew larger and benefited from improved weaponry and overseas campaign experience – while the Highland way of life slowly eroded.

If ever a people had the dice loaded against their survival, it was the highlanders. They were a bastion of tribalism in a country that was undergoing an irreversible process of modernisation. Their very existence depended on holing up in the highlands and keeping quiet. Launching a full-scale attack on the rest of that country was the last thing they needed to do.

And that is exactly what they did.

It would be nice to think that, in his heart, the highlander decided to go out in a blaze of glory because he knew his way of life was doomed. But no matter what the reasons for it, another uprising was going to be the stuff of legend. There was never any doubt that the man who led the last great rebellion would go down in history.

In 1740 the War of Austrian Succession broke out in Europe, putting

Britain and France, once again, on opposing sides. For the first time in many years, Louis of France thought it might be a good idea to support a Jacobite uprising in Scotland and put the northern wolf back at England's door. James Stuart, however, was now unhealthy and weak-willed. Though he loved to plot the regaining of his father's throne, it was obvious he was going nowhere.

James VII's grandson, however, was a different matter.

Charles Edward Stuart was confident, charming and handsome – the perfect choice to rekindle the dying embers of the Jacobite cause – and it is for these qualities that he is remembered in story and song. But Charles was also headstrong, petulant and irresponsible – just what was needed to doom that cause from the beginning.

Charles travelled from Rome, where his family were in exile, to help command a French invasion fleet massing to invade Britain. The Royal Navy, however, were on to this plan and the combination of a British blockage and severe weather caused the invasion to be abandoned. Charles decided, wrongly, that French assistance would be forthcoming if he initiated a Jacobite rising on his own. It was the first of many arrogant blunders fuelled by an inability to distinguish what he *wanted* to happen from what was really *going* to happen (not an uncommon tendency among the European aristocracy at the time).

The French certainly weren't going to stop Charles's venture, but offered him little support. Charles didn't even tell his own father of his plans to land in Scotland with a token force and raise support there. With good reason. A long time had passed since the last uprising and this expedition by the 'Young Pretender' was by far the most ill-planned and under-funded of all the Jacobite ventures.

In 1745, Charles Edward Stuart landed on the shores of Scotland with a

small group of followers – including John O'Sullivan, a mediocre Irish officer whom Charles came to value more than men he really needed. The young prince did not get the massive support he had hoped for in Scotland. Although he quickly gathered a Jacobite army, it was not the vast one he had dreamed of. His greatest asset in the coming campaign was to be Lord George Murray (1694–1760), a distinguished military campaigner and a fine strategist.

Murray had great reservations about participating in the Jacobite campaign, a venture he felt was doomed from the start, and he and Charles were not impressed with each other. Murray was haughty, did not suffer fools gladly and lumped most of the prince's other advisors into that category – especially John O'Sullivan. Murray admitted that he was jeopardising 'my life, my future, my expectations [and] the happiness of my wife and children' by joining Charles. On the other hand, he felt that 'honour and my duty to King and Country outweighs everything'.

He reluctantly agreed to throw in his hand with the prince. Despite his prickly persona, Murray understood how to use both the strengths and weaknesses of the Highland fighter to their best advantage, and was prepared to lead them from the front when necessary. He took an irregular and motley group of pugilists and quickly made them into a fighting force that rocked the British nation.

The Jacobites marched south, took Edinburgh, and then scored a major military victory at Prestonpans. Murray, without consulting Charles, raced to gain the high ground opposite General Cope's approaching government army. A skilful flanking manoeuvre and a well-timed Highland charge through the morning mist destroyed the opposition and sent them fleeing.

Heartened by this, the Jacobite leaders agreed to invade England, though the decision was far from unanimous – it was only carried by one vote. Murray favoured remaining in Scotland and building up a strong defensive army that would encourage the French to send support. There are many historians who have pointed out the impracticality of such a 'Fortress Scotland' policy, insisting that the blockading power of the Royal Navy would have stopped the French and the financial strength of the south would have destroyed Scotland. Perhaps that is true. What we do know is that the course the Jacobites did follow led to their annihilation and the destruction of the Highlands.

Nothing, surely, could be worse than that.

Many of the senior Jacobites advocated dissolving the union and making Scotland an independent country again – with Charles as their king. Had the Young Pretender felt any real loyalty to the men who had risen for him, he might have considered this plan. But Charles had no desire to be only the King of Scotland. He wanted the throne of Britain.

In hindsight, there should be no real surprise at this. Though Bonnie Prince Charlie is usually depicted as a tartan-wearing lover of all things Scottish, this was hardly the case – he adopted Highland dress, for example, only after arriving in Scotland. Charles was born in Europe, as was his father, and his grandfather and great-grandfather were born and lived in England. There was nothing Scottish about Charles Edward Stuart except his name.

Charles was willing to do anything to get his chance at conquering

Britain and deliberately misled his own followers to achieve that aim. He told his chief advisors that he was personally in touch with prominent English Jacobites who would rise when his troops marched south. In fact, Charles had done very little to rally support south of the border.

Nor was Charles Stuart in close contact with the French government, as he claimed. He insisted that French troops would land in force to support the Jacobite cause with no proof that this would actually happen. In fact, looking at the past record of French support for Scotland, it would have been highly unrealistic to assume the Jacobites would receive overseas aid. Had Charles remained in the north and built up a significant Scottish following, there might have been a chance that Louis would have tried to land on the shores of his ally. But co-ordinating an attack on London from Scotland and France was too problematical to be within the realms of possibility.

It's also hard to imagine that any Englishmen would rise to support an invading Scots force backed by a French army – the traditional enemy of England.

There is no denying the bravery and sheer audacity of the Young Pretender's efforts, but there is little doubt that the best interests of his men were not at the forefront of his mind.

The Jacobite army that eventually crossed the border into England

numbered only 5,500. More troops were being raised in Scotland but, if there was to be a push on London, there was no time to wait for them. This was a woefully small number with which to attempt the conquest of an entire country, but the Jacobites turned out to be quite a surprise to those they encountered. Traditionally each Highland clan had formed its own fighting unit but, under Lord Murray, the 1745 force had been organised into proper regiments and companies – something resembling a real army.

The Jacobites besieged Carlisle and took the city with comparative ease, then marched south again at a speed that caught the British government on the hop. Charles, a keen sportsman, was young and very fit – enabling him to march at the head of a force that could cover thirty miles a day. The hardy Scots would, no doubt, have appreciated this ability.

The Jacobites had always intended to capture London, but Murray managed to keep the Hanoverian forces guessing as to their final destination. The British government panicked and ordered the Duke of Cumberland and his entire overseas army back to Britain – swelling the Hanoverian forces to 30,000 troops.

Murray marched the Jacobites west towards Wales and Cumberland moved to intercept him, drawing up his army to meet an attack that never happened. Murray's march west had been a feint. He was now heading south-east again and had bypassed Cumberland's force entirely. The wily Jacobite commander had out-thought and out-manoeuvred the government troops and, on 4 December 1745, Murray reached the city of Derby.

It was here that a fateful decision was made. Lord Murray had seen little evidence of English Jacobite support and argued that no military strategy would now allow Charles to win in the south. By turning back, at least the army they had could be saved. The Highland chiefs, horrified at the distance their small army found itself from Scotland, agreed wholeheartedly. The Jacobites were dealt a final blow when a Hanoverian spy, named Dudley Bradstreet, convinced them there was a government army waiting to intercept them at London.

This was not true, but both Murray and Charles Stuart believed it, and their reaction to the news was very different. Murray insisted that, even if they beat this army and took London, their force would be reduced to a tiny, battle-weary group who wouldn't stand a chance of holding the capital. There were no French forces, no Jacobite support in England and, even worse, there would be an army led by General Wade and another headed by Cumberland between them and their home.

Murray saw no way of winning in these circumstances, and believed that defeat would surely lead to Jacobite annihilation: the survivors would never make it back to Scotland across hundreds of miles of enemy country. The only solution was to retreat to Scotland. There the Jacobites could build up their army properly, wait for French aid and plan their next campaign. The fact that they had performed so magnificently must surely impress upon the French, and the Scots who had stayed neutral, that the Jacobites were in with a fighting chance.

Charles Stuart was having none of it. If they could just reach London, he argued, the government would surely collapse and the English Jacobites would rise *en masse*. When challenged to provide proof of this, Charles was forced to admit he had lied about his support south of the border. Any chance he had of using charm to convince the highlanders to keep advancing faded drastically at this point.

In Scots legend, Murray had always been treated harshly for insisting on retreat when the Jacobites were so close to their goal. Charles, on the other hand, has been applauded for his courageous insistence that the Jacobites keep going. Jacobite enthusiasts have pointed out that, since there was no army between the prince and London, Charles was right – he *could* have taken the capital of Britain.

This argument misses the point. Both Charles and Lord Murray believed in Bradstreet's army. Acting on the knowledge they had, to go forward would have been suicidal. Besides, the object of the Jacobite cause was not simply to take London; it was to overthrow the Hanoverian dynasty. Marching an insignificant force of highlanders into the capital with no support and 30,000 Hanoverian troops in hot pursuit was never going to achieve that goal.

Realising the hopelessness of their situation, Murray simply made the best of a bad lot. It would certainly have looked good to reach London, but it would have ended in his own men being massacred, and he wasn't going to let that happen. The fact that they *were* massacred at Culloden is beside the point – if Charles had listened to Murray at that particular battle they might not have been.

Charles Edward Stewart, on the other hand, didn't seem to care if his highlanders didn't make it back. This was his one good shot at the throne and he was aware that only astonishing luck had got him this far. He was willing to gamble the lives of all of his men that his luck would hold. The men, whose lives he was gambling with, didn't share his optimism. Many had followed him out of conviction in the Stuart cause, not the belief that they would win. Others were just along for the fight. Whatever their reasons, suicide wasn't part of the bargain.

The demoralised troops began the march back north, trekking across hostile territory and trying to avoid the Hanoverian armies. Whereas he had walked at the front of his army on the way south, Charles now withdrew into himself. Despite the prompting of his advisors he stopped communicating with his troops and appeared to suffer bouts of psychosomatic illness.

Though the prince pouted and sulked when faced with adversity, it brought out the best in Lord Murray – at Clifton, his rearguard action drove off Cumberland's troops and allowed the Jacobites some respite at Carlisle.

At Carlisle, Charles insisted that a garrison of troops be left to hold the town until he returned. Murray protested that this would be a waste of good men and reminded Charles of how easily the Jacobites had taken the town. Charles insisted. The garrison lasted only ten days.

Back in Scotland, Charles seemed to have lost sight of exactly what he wanted to do and besieged Stirling more for the sake of it than for any real military objective. There the Jacobites stayed until the Hanoverian army, commanded by Henry Hawley, caught up with them.

Charles and his leaders drew up the Jacobite army to fight the government forces just outside Stirling, but Murray had a better plan. He suggested a surprise attack at Falkirk instead. It was the last thing the Hanoverian troops expected – Hawley hadn't even bothered to send out cavalry patrols. The Jacobite army roared into battle and broke the Hanoverian ranks. Once again that great Highland charge, led by Lord Murray, had done the trick. After the battle, Murray pressed for Hawley to be pursued while his troops were still in chaos – undoubtedly the best course of action to take. The prince, however, was determined to take Stirling Castle and allowed Hawley's army to reach Edinburgh and regroup.

Cumberland had been recalled to England but was now speedily despatched to Scotland to take command of the government forces again. Murray had devised a plan for meeting him in battle but the Highland chiefs, alarmed at how many highlanders were returning to their homes, insisted on retreating north to build up the Jacobite army again. Charles, wrongly, believed that Murray was behind this and the relationship between the two men worsened. The Jacobites moved to the northern Highlands while Cumberland made camp in Aberdeen to wait out the winter.

By this time Charles Stuart seemed to have lost all interest in the campaign. When he wasn't ill, or depressed, he spent his time hunting on the moors. When spring arrived, Cumberland moved towards the static Jacobite camp and a final confrontation.

Murray wanted to fight near Dalcross Castle where rough ground would give the highlanders maximum protection from the Hanoverian artillery. O'Sullivan, however, preferred the flat ground of Culloden Moor and Charles Stuart agreed with him. Murray objected strongly and even suggested fighting a guerrilla war rather than a battle. Again he was overruled. For the first and only time in the campaign, Prince Charles Edward Stuart took personal command of the Jacobite army.

The prince and O'Sullivan came up with the idea of a surprise night attack, thinking that the Hanoverians could be caught off guard as they celebrated Cumberland's birthday. Murray didn't like this notion either, but reluctantly agreed, since anything was better than fighting on Culloden Moor. The highlanders, however, had more than eight miles of boggy terrain to cross in the dark – and had to keep halting for the small French force with them to catch up. When dawn began to rise, the Jacobites were still two miles from Cumberland's position.

The prince, at the rear, ordered Murray's front column to press on and attack. Knowing that this suicidal move would accomplish nothing, Murray refused. The Jacobites retreated back to Culloden in disarray – starving, exhausted and demoralised. Cumberland, with well-equipped and freshly rested troops, followed them.

For the first time the Jacobite army encountered well-disciplined troops – backed by cavalry and artillery – facing them across ground perfect for the kind of battle Cumberland wished to fight. Decimated early on by the enemy's cannon fire, the Jacobites had no choice but to charge.

They never stood a chance. Cumberland had placed his most experienced men in the front line and all the Hanoverian infantry had been trained in new techniques for combat against the sword-wielding highlanders.

The prince, realising the battle was lost, turned and left the battlefield – minutes after screaming that he would never be taken alive. Though his retreat may have been at the urging of his advisors, the normally headstrong prince found this particular advice easy to follow, much to the disgust of some of his commanders. It is reported that Lord Elcho shouted after him 'There you go, you cowardly Italian'.

The undying loyalty of his men was being sorely tested.

Even then the Jacobites were willing to wage a guerrilla war. On the

desolate moors and mountains the highlanders knew so well, they would still have been a formidable adversary. Charles, however, decided to return to security in France. He wrote to Lord George Murray advising every man to look to his own safety.

This unexpected blow was the last straw for Murray, who already had 4,000 men gathered at Ruthven ready to continue fighting. He wrote a bitter reply, charging the prince with betraying his own men, and disbanded the disillusioned army.

Lord Murray and Charles Stuart never met again.

Cumberland unleashed his soldiers on the north with a barbarity that shocked even the highlanders. Hunted like criminals, even those clans who had not fought for Charles found themselves crushed by government oppression.

They were a broken people.

For the next five months Prince Charles Edward Stuart was a fugitive – and it was from this point that the prince's reputation as a bona fide Scottish hero was cemented. It is generally considered that his courage, wit and resourcefulness allowed him to survive where other men would have given in or been captured. However, Charles was an exceptionally fit young man and, unless he wanted to spend the rest of his life in prison, it's difficult to see what else he could have done. After all, living rough was nothing out of the ordinary for the average highlander and there were hundreds of other Jacobites in the same boat (though, admittedly, not as wanted as Charles). The area where the outlawed prince travelled was actually more populated in the early eighteenth century than it is today and some Jacobites remained hidden for years. Charles had never set foot in Scotland until 1745 and depended entirely on the resourcefulness and local knowledge of a small number of companions to get him from place to place.

As it was, he began to drink heavily – a bottle of brandy a day – and made more than one selfish decision, against the advice of his followers, that almost resulted in their death or capture – including insisting on taking a boat out into a storm and sending his own men into townships when he was not sure if they would be arrested.

Despite a massive reward of £30,000 for his capture, no highlander turned Charles Edward Stuart over to the government. However, this is as much a reflection on the highlanders' loyalty, and their hatred of Cumberland's genocidal policy, as a comment on the prince's popularity.

Eventually, with the help of his small band of followers, and the reluctant participation of Flora MacDonald (following her sense of duty rather than her heart), Bonnie Prince Charlie escaped to France and to legend. The rest of Charles's life was a sad shadow of his year of glory. France made peace with Britain in 1748 and Charles was forced to leave the country and return to Italy. By the 1750s he was prone to fits of uncontrollable rage whenever he was crossed. Always cold with women, he started to become violent towards them.

He died in 1788, a bitter alcoholic, and is buried in Rome. Bonnie Prince Charlie has become one of the great mythical figures of

Scottish history – and even those who accept his flaws still find the need to point out his charm and ability to lead men. David Morgan, an executed English Jacobite described Charles as having a character that 'exceeds anything I could have imagined or conceived. An attempt to describe him would seem gross flattery.'

Obviously an impressionable man.

There is no doubt that the young Charles Edward Stuart possessed charm by the bucketload, but charm and athletic handsomeness were pretty much all he had going for him – and he didn't always use the former quality. Unlike Lord Murray, he simply did not have what it took to pull off such a momentous undertaking. The Chevalier de Johnstone famously remarked that if the Prince had been asleep during the campaign, and left everything to Lord Murray, he would have woken with the crowns of Great Britain on his head!

Charles didn't need good qualities to command the loyalty of his men. The Jacobites followed their prince without question, even when he was at his most incompetent and petulant. He was the rightful king and that was that. Like so many generations of Scots before them, this fact was enough for the Jacobites. The king's personal attributes did not come into it.

Over the years, however, the notion has taken hold that Charles inspired devotion by being a cross between Robert Redford and a tartan Napoleon. This takes away from the real heroism of the highlanders. Their loyalty was to a cause, not to a man. That's why the campaign of 1745 is so important to Scotland. Scots from all parts of the country rarely fought for any other reason than love of fighting and getting their hands on booty. But this time a group of Scots were battling for something that could be called noble – to right what they saw was a great wrong. They did it despite overwhelming odds. And, though they paid a horrendous price for it, they would not betray the man they fought for.

No wonder Bonnie Prince Charlie has become a legend. As the

figurehead of such an uncharacteristic Scots movement, he could hardly have become anything else.

But men like Lord Murray and his highlanders – who charged an army at Culloden they knew they couldn't possibly defeat – are the real heroes of the 1745 rebellion. They fought and died for their own beliefs, not for the fantasy of Charles Edward Stuart.

In that respect only Charles Edward Stuart lost. The highlanders did not.

There is an interesting footnote to the Bonnie Prince Charlie story. It is

generally regarded that the true Stuart line ended with the death of Charles's brother Henry in 1807. This, however, is not the case.

In 1647 Charles Stuart – Charles II of Britain – had a child, Prince Giacomo Enrico de Boveria Rohana-Stuardo. He died in Naples in 1669 (though a poplar rival theory states that he was imprisoned for life instead – giving rise to the story *The Man in the Iron Mask*), but his widow bore him a posthumous son, Prince Giacomo Stuardo of Naples. Giacomo led a long and tempestuous life in Germany and Italy and in 1722 had a son named Prince Joseph Stuart de Roehenstart – who actually fought with Bonnie Prince Charlie during the 1745 rebellion. After the failure of Culloden, Joseph Stuart returned to France on the same boat as Charles and settled at Kilvala in Brittany.

Thanks to the research of the historian George Washington, it has now been established that Joseph Stuart too had a son, named Prince Augustus Edward Maximilian de Roehenstart – also known as Dr Ferdinand Smyth-Stuart. Smyth-Stuart's life was an unremarkable one except for one thing.

He married Charlotte Stuart, Duchess of Albany, the daughter of Bonnie Prince Charlie. In 1781, they had a son. That son, Charles Edward Stewart, Count of Roehenstart was descended from Stuart kings on both sides of his family and as such was the rightful heir to the throne of Britain.

Fascinating as this fact is, it has a rather anti-climactic conclusion. Charles Stuart de Roehenstart, the 'New Pretender', never even tried to claim the British throne. He died, after falling off a horse, in 1854. Yet there is a more intriguing side to the story of the Stuart lineage – and it involves one of the most famous men in history.

There are no less than three separate theories to suggest that the diminutive, aggressive French military mastermind, Emperor Napoleon Bonaparte, was directly descended from Scots. Two of these theories point to his descent from the royal Stuarts themselves.

One is a theory that Prince Giacomo Enrico de Boveria Rohana-Stuardo, the man in the iron mask, had a second son while incarcerated in the bay of Cannes. The boy was smuggled away to Corsica where he was given the name of 'de buona parte' – of good family. The boy became the grandfather of the famous Napoleon.

There is also evidence that the emperor's grandmother, Mme Maria Bonaparte, had a love affair in Ajaccio, Corsica, with Prince Joseph Stuart de Roehenstart (1722–83) – and that their child was Napoleon's father.

If either theory is correct, Napoleon was descended from the royal line of Stuarts. The Frenchman himself often hinted that he was of royal lineage.

The last theory is that Napoleon's grandfather was William Bayne from the Scottish village of Balloch! After the 1745 Jacobite rebellion, Bayne and his family were forced to leave Scotland, but their ship sank in the Mediterranean, leaving the family stranded on Corsica. The name Bayne became corrupted to Boun and the family became known as the 'Boun party' – or Boun-de-partie!

The Jacobites followed one fated European leader to destruction – but it seems, because of this, they may have created a far more successful one.

FIVE NATIONS

Three miles from us across the river Captain Currie's farm is possessed by two Allans from Edinburgh; two miles below him is Mr Kinghorn's from Teviotdale, 5,000 acres. The next is Captain Ross's splendid property and house and then Howie's and J.J. Moore's . . .

AUSTRALIAN SETTLER DAVID WAUGH, DESCRIBING
A PREPONDERANCE OF SCOTTISH NEIGHBOURS IN THE 1830S

The Scots were not popular abroad: that has pretty much been established already. This did not mean that their influence was inconsequential – in fact, it was enormous. In the United States, for instance, Scots were instrumental in the development of the US mining industry, cattle ranching and large-scale agriculture.

The 'Highland Clearances' are a famous chapter in history. No country has ever lost so large a percentage of its native population. Yet most people do not realise that this mass exodus continued until very recently: 1,388,000 Scots emigrated between 1901 and 1961, more than one-fifth of the country's entire population.

The more current emigrations of Scots have not had the global impact of their forefathers, but then the world is not so easy to shape these days. And modern Scots seem to have lost many of the characteristics that made them so unpopular, yet so successful – a mixed blessing surely.

Evidence of Scotland's former influence, however, is found all over the globe. For example, there are 14 Aberdeens in the world and Scotsmen are celebrated in Russia, Japan, Chile, Australia and the US as founders of their respective navies.

Often, the lone Scottish entrepreneur has had a profound effect on his adopted country while remaining unknown in his homeland.

Thomas Blake Glover of Fraserburgh (1838–1911), a nonentity in Scotland, is famous in Japan – every year over two million Japanese visit his mansion in Nagasaki – the most popular tourist attraction in the country. Originally employed by the Scots trading company of Jardine Matheson, he struck out on his own with spectacular success. He was instrumental in transforming Japan from an archaic feudal system into an industrial power: he opened the country's first coal mine and imported its first locomotive and shipping dock. He went on to found the Japanese navy and the giant Mitsubishi Corporation. He also added a bit of colour to the normally reserved Japanese society, by fathering an impressive number of children and having an affair that became the inspiration for Puccini's *Madame Butterfly*.

In 1908, Japan's emperor awarded Glover the Order of the Rising Sun.

In India, two Scots named Hugh Falconer (1808–65) and William Jamieson were chiefly responsible for the development of tea plantations. Mountstuart Elphinstone (1779–1859) shaped the state education system of India and Samuel Laing was India's first finance minister. Allan Octavian Hume founded the Indian Congress Party and is known (in India, of course) as the father of the Indian National Congress – a party which has assumed an almost continuous supremacy over independent India's political life.

In Russia, General Patrick Gordon (1635–99), from Aberdeen, became admiral and chief military advisor to Peter the Great. None too fond of the place to begin with, he was 'persuaded' to stay by the possibility of ending up in Siberia if he tried to leave and eventually became the Tsar's right-hand man. When Peter took a trip to the West, Gordon was left in charge of the Kremlin, and saved the Tsar's reign by suppressing a rebellion. When Gordon died, another Scotsman, James Bruce, became Peter's new adviser, while his brother repulsed three Swedish assaults to become the 'Saviour of St Petersburg'.

Katharine the Great said of her Scottish military commander, James Keith (1696–1758): 'I had sooner lose 10,000 of my best soldiers than Keith'. She also called the Scotsman 'the only man who can bring up a future heir of the throne in my mind and in the footsteps of Peter the Great'. Keith saw exactly where this would lead and wrote to a friend: 'The Empress is resolved to raise me to a height which would cause my ruin as well as her own.' He promptly fled to Prussia where Fredrick the Great made him Governor of Berlin.

Two countries more than any other, however, have been moulded by the Scots: Canada and Australia.

Canada has links with Scotland which go back to antiquity. In 1010 AD, when Thorfinn Karlsevni explored the coast of Canada, two Scots were reported to have been among his crew and in 1542 Jean Rotz, son of Scotsman David Ross, was one of the first men to map the St Lawrence river.

In the early corridors of power, the Scots stood wall to wall. Though they numbered only one fifteenth of the population, Scots dominated the government and controlled the fur trade, the educational institutions and the banks. In Quebec, the ruling government body was so dominated by Scots that it was called the 'Scotch Party'.

The Scots lack of class-consciousness allowed them to treat the Indians better than other immigrants and their Auld Alliance led to good relations with the numerous French settlers. As usual, they quickly replaced their predecessors and by 1799, four out of every five employees in the Hudson Bay Company were Scottish. The unflinching steadfastness of these Scots immigrants turned the Hudson Bay Company into the largest corporate landowner in history – an empire covering 3 million square miles of Canada and the US, with 110 forts stretched along the way.

Just how deeply the Scots infiltrated this massive continent was illustrated by a visit by the Canadian Governor-General (a Scot) to an outpost in the Canadian wilderness. When the inquisitive official asked to be introduced to a bunch of menacing-looking Indians, the post manager (also a Scot) beckoned to one of the savages with the immortal words, 'Would ye come here for a minute, MacDonald?'

As Canada moved from a colony to a nation, the Scots were at the forefront of development. The first two prime ministers of Canada were born in Scotland, the Canadian Pacific railway was designed, financed and built mainly by Scots and the Canadian banking and business systems, still used today, were based on their Scottish counterparts. Five of the first six colleges in Canada were founded by Scots, as was the Canadian National Film Board. Still on the entertainment front, a Scottish chemist concocted Canada Dry Ginger Ale in the 1800s.

According to Professor T.W. Acheson, in the years between 1880 and 1885, 20 per cent of the industrial elite of Canada was born in Scotland and 28 per cent had Scots fathers. The total of 48 per cent is even more astonishing, considering that only 3 per cent of the population were first or second generation Scots.

The fledgling nation of Australia saw similar early manipulation, as one might expect when so many rebellious Scots ended up getting sent there. John Macarthur (1767–1834), the son of Argyllshire parents, introduced the Marino sheep into Australia and is considered the founder of Australia's gigantic sheep industry. This was rather an ironic move considering his own clan had been replaced by the sheep's woolly counterparts back home. With equal foresight, Macarthur planted the country's first vineyard, starting an industry much more palatable to the Scots.

These innovations made Macarthur the most powerful man in this developing community – his power matched that of Australia's Scottish Governor, John Hunter.

Hunter was an able, conscientious and courageous man, dedicated to lessening the abusive power of the military and transferring it to civil government. In this he was bitterly opposed by Macarthur, who was doing a roaring trade with the armed forces.

The rigid hold that Britain maintained over the former penal colony was weakened further by another Scot, Robert Campbell, who broke the monopoly of the giant East India Company to become the country's first independent trader.

Seeing that things down-under were getting out of hand, the British government recalled John Hunter and appointed a new Australian governor, none other than William Bligh of *Mutiny on the Bounty* fame. Applying the same subtle techniques that had landed him in a lifeboat a few years earlier, Bligh implemented a régime of misadministration and harshness. The result was just as predictable – a mutiny. A Scotsman named Major George Johnstone imprisoned Bligh, then sent him back to England – surely the first time that anyone had been deported *out* of Australia. Governorship was taken over by yet another Scot, William Paterson.

This time the British government took no chances. In 1810, they sent a highlander, Lachlan Macquarrie (1762–1824) to be the next Australian Governor, accompanied by the 73rd Highlanders of the Black Watch.

Macquarrie was less than impressed by what he saw. In his opinion the colony was 'barely emerging from infantile imbecility'. He instigated a public-works programme, provided public buildings including a library, encouraged exploration, built roads, set out the layout for the city of Sydney and discouraged discrimination against ex-convicts and Aborigines. He even appointed a Poet Laureate – the very thing a former penal colony was crying out for.

When he left in 1821, Macquarrie had transformed this unruly and disorganised colony of ex-convicts into a civilised and thriving community, and earned himself the title of the 'Father of Australia'. He was replaced as Governor by yet another Scot, Thomas Brisbane – a name familiar to most Australians.

Brisbane introduced tobacco plants and sugar cane, along with freedom of the press and encouraged an influx of settlers. Now people actually chose to go to Australia instead of just being sent there.

Fittingly, the Scots influence down-under is forever marked by one of the high points of Australian culture. Andrew Paterson, the son of a Scottish immigrant, wrote 'Waltzing Matilda'.

THE POETS CORNERED

We rose on the wave with songs. We rushed with joy, through the foam of the deep.

OSSIAN, *FINGAL*

Who is the most famous Scottish poet of all time? Robert Burns? He certainly is now, but there was a time when the creator of 'Auld Lang Syne' was easily overshadowed by another Scottish poet – the ancient bard, Ossian. Lost for half a millennium, the works of this seminal Celtic poet were rediscovered in 1760 and received phenomenal critical and commercial success. He may not be a household name these days but, amazingly, Ossian was the most popular poet in Europe in the eighteenth century and vied with Byron for top billing in the nineteenth century as well.

Ossian's melancholy epics of fated warriors and doomed loves played a major role in bringing about the Romantic Movement in European Literature. Oscar Wilde's mother gave her son the middle name Fingal after an Ossianic poem and Napoleon took an Italian copy of Ossian's works on all his campaigns.

Ossian's verses captivated the great minds of Europe for half a century and influenced the likes of Schiller, Coleridge, Scott, Byron, Hogg, Diderot, Massanet, Schubert and Mendelssohn. Even the great English pastoral poet, Thomas Gray, raved that he had 'gone mad about them'.

The huge impact of Ossian was felt not only in Europe: Thomas Jefferson was so affected by the ancient Scottish writer that he attempted to learn Gaelic and declared, 'I am not ashamed to own that I think this rude bard of the North the greatest Poet that has ever existed.'

After the publication of Ossian's writings, visitors poured into Scotland to witness the sights the bard described, helping to open up the north. Walter Scott drew heavily on Ossian's work and became even more influential in shaping the world perception of Scotland's past. Though he may not be famous now, Ossian's images of ancient Scotland have found themselves a little niche in the world's subconscious.

Ossian *is* the voice of ancient Scotland.

Which is a shame, really, because Ossian didn't exist. His poetry is the work of an eighteenth century highlander named James Macpherson.

Born in 1736, Macpherson (1736–96) grew up in the Gaelic-speaking area of rural Badenoch, half a mile from Ruthven Barracks. Ruthven was a military outpost, keeping an eye on Highland clans whom the British government still feared and mistrusted. Despite the proximity of the soldiers, the Macphersons were very much part of the clan system and James grew up with a thorough knowledge of Highland folk mythology.

When Prince Charles Edward Stuart landed in Scotland in 1745 to begin the Jacobite rebellion, the Macpherson clan joined his cause and burned Ruthven Barracks. Their victory was short lived. Bonnie Prince Charlie's highlanders were annihilated at Culloden the next year and the Macphersons were one of the clans who were systematically hounded by government troops.

James Macpherson, fortunately, escaped this sorry situation when his intellectual abilities secured him a place at Aberdeen University. There, under the tutelage of the classics scholar Thomas Blackwell, Macpherson learned about the societies of the ancient world. He read about the trials of Homeric heroes and how the savage German tribes used their strength and courage to overrun the mighty Roman Empire. Surrounded by these influences, Macpherson had no problem in seeing the epic possibilities in the struggles faced by his own Highland relations. Remembering the stories from his childhood, he could easily see, in the history of his nation, an unending line of heroes moulded by such titanic efforts.

Inspired by these ideas, he returned to teach at Ruthven School after graduation, and began avidly collecting local ballads and tales.

In 1759, Macpherson met the historian John Home (1722-1808) at a bowling green in Moffat – an encounter that was a major turning point in the young teacher's life. Home was an established literary figure and, more importantly, interested in collecting Scottish folklore. He was delighted at finding this 6' 3" highlander: a collector of Gaelic tales who was also a classical scholar and immediately began pressing Macpherson to translate something Gaelic for him to print.

Macpherson was reluctant at first, but eventually 'translated' a piece called *The Death of Oscar*. Home took the work to Dr Hugh Blair, the literary arbiter of Edinburgh and together they decided they had a literary revelation of great antiquity and rare genius. They printed the piece as part of a small volume entitled *Fragments of Ancient Poetry collected in the Highlands of Scotland*.

Fragments was a major hit with the press and public alike. The prose was simple, rhythmic and powerful and readers felt they were really seeing ancient Scotland through the eyes of its Celtic warriors.

The interest of the nation was piqued. Were there more of these Scottish works to be recovered from obscurity? The preface to *Fragments* suggested that there were:

> It is to be believed that, by careful inquiry, many more remains of ancient genius, no less valuable than those now given to the world, might be found in the same country where these have been collected. In particular there is reason to hope that one work of considerable length, and which deserves to be styled an heroic poem, might be discovered and translated.

If anyone was going to discover and translate an ancient heroic Scots poem, James Macpherson seemed the man for the job. He had confided to Edinburgh literary figures that there were still old men in the Highlands who could repeat this lost epic from memory – and soon found himself dispatched north to find them.

Macpherson found a lot more than he bargained for. As he journeyed through the Highlands and Islands of Scotland, everyone he came across seemed to have a tale to tell. To quote Henry Graham: 'venerable blacksmiths and sons of bards, recited long screeds of Fingalian verse in high nasal accents with the prospective reward of a gill of whiskey or a roll of tobacco'. Within weeks Macpherson had bags full of stories, poems and ballads.

Anyone who has played Chinese whispers will appreciate the magnitude of Macpherson's task and what he actually did with these sackloads has been the subject of controversy ever since. What *is* known is that Macpherson returned after four months to report that an ancient Scottish epic had been retrieved. A blind Celtic bard called Ossian, on a level with Homer himself, had been uncovered after 1,300 years in the poetic wilderness.

In 1761, the results of Macpherson's search were published under the titles *Fingal: An Ancient Epic Poem in Six Books. Together with several Other Poems composed by Ossian the Son of Fingal* and the equally catchy *Temore: An ancient Epic Poem in Eight Books. Together with several Other poems composed by Ossian the Son of Fingal.*

The books were a literary sensation and translated into German, French, Italian, Danish, Swedish, Polish and Russian. All of Europe was fascinated by life in ancient Scotland told first hand. Macpherson, the modest highlander, had originally been reluctant to take on such a daunting task. Now he surrendered to the lure of being a celebrity.

It didn't suit him. Once a shy and likeable man, he became so insufferable that David Hume declared he had never met anyone 'more perverse and unamiable'.

Macpherson was resentful at being called a translator rather than a poet and, in hindsight, it's easy to see why he got so miffed. He wasn't a mere translator. He had written huge chunks of the most famous and acclaimed text in Europe himself – and he wasn't able to tell anyone about it.

But misgivings about the authenticity of Macpherson's discovery finally began to surface. The poet James Beattie and the philosopher David Hume – always one for empirical evidence – suggested that Macpherson might like to produce the originals he had supposedly translated. In retort Macpherson placed 'original' Gaelic manuscripts in a London bookshop as proof for anyone to inspect. Since nobody in London could read Gaelic, they remained undisputed until Macpherson withdrew them again.

The redoubtable Samuel Johnson then joined the fray, openly criticising Ossian as a fake. Macpherson wrote a furious letter informing Johnson that 'his age and his infirmities alone protected him from the treatment due to an infamous liar'. Johnson took Macpherson at his word and began carrying a six foot cudgel for protection.

The more suspicion grew, the more Macpherson blustered, refusing to admit that he had made anything up. Yet an analysis of the *Works of Ossian* reveals massive flaws. There are chronological impossibilities and geographical errors. There are customs the ancients never practised and descriptions of armour they never wore. Scottish and Irish heroes mingle freely or bear the wrong names. (Macpherson refused to believe that the Scots originally came from Ireland.)

The beleaguered highlander turned to other literary pursuits, translating the *Iliad* in three months flat and writing a *History of Great Britain*, which was pilloried by Hume as 'the most wretched production that ever came from his press'.

Hume really didn't like Macpherson much.

James Macpherson died in 1765, taking his secrets to the grave – when his personal belongings were investigated no Ossianic documents were found. An investigative committee was set up by the Highland Society of Scotland to try and ascertain how much of Ossian's work was real and how much was imagination. They concluded that, though some of the work was original – old Scots tales were clearly recognisable – Macpherson had liberally embellished the stories and added passages of his own whenever he considered that the material wasn't quite as epic as it ought to be. The prose, too, while indebted to the style of Gaelic Scotland, was definitely Macpherson's own.

Despite this, Macpherson had his champions. Such noted figures as Lord Kames and the novelist Henry Mackenzie insisted that Ossian's work was a genuine translation of a third century Gaelic epic and the public were reluctant to accept that they had been duped. The fact that some of Ossian's works arose from genuine material meant that Macpherson escaped widespread condemnation: 'poetic licence' was much more acceptable to the population than the 'translator' simply making everything up.

Besides, the works of Ossian were a cracking good read. Though most Scots would be reluctant to admit it, they're probably a lot more epic, heroic and generally better told than any originals would have been.

In the end, however, the weight of evidence was against Macpherson and his works fell from massive popularity to relative obscurity. But it was too late to stop myth replacing fact. Ossian's portrayal of the Scots warrior as Heathcliff in a kilt was accepted all over the world.

There is no denying that the works of Macpherson/Ossian are an incredible accomplishment – the poetry is stirring and well written and, in recent years, has enjoyed something of a renaissance. The scholar Fiona Stafford has defended Macpherson, arguing that to call his work fake is 'to ignore the complexities of Macpherson's achievement and indeed the circumstances under which he worked'.

There is no doubt that Macpherson's achievements are impressive and it is true that, in creating, we all draw on various influences. We cannot, however, deny those influences entirely and claim to be the original. Macpherson was supposed to be a translator, not a storyteller. Much as he wanted to tell the ancient stories dramatically, he didn't tell them honestly.

Macpherson may have been a highlander but he was also a classically trained eighteenth century scholar, not a third century bard. His 'true' stories were really inventions.

If we pretend they were not, we are faking Scottish history as much as he did.

> The sons of the feeble hereafter will lift the voice on Cona; and looking up to the rocks, say 'Here Ossian dwelt.' They shall admire the chiefs of old, and the race that are no more . . .

WE, THE PEOPLE

Every line of strength in American history is a line coloured with Scottish blood.

WOODROW WILSON, US PRESIDENT

Other European countries had established dominance in various parts of North America long before the Scots had any real presence in the colonies. One of the strongest influences was, not surprisingly, England, and, by the eighteenth century, English philosophy had become dominant in North America.

However, the fervent stirring of creativity which was happening in Scotland would soon be carried by thousands of Scots immigrants to their new home. As settlers, the Scots may have been disliked, but their outlook as a general group was far less class-conscious than that of their southern neighbours and this appealed greatly to other colonial settlers, many of whom had moved to America to escape persecution.

By the time of the American Revolution, thanks to the Scottish Enlightenment back home, the ideas of Scotland's foremost thinkers were being discussed all over the globe. Edinburgh, the 'Athens of the

North', was the envy of the world for intellect. Glasgow held an equivalent position in industry. The poetry of Burns, the paintings of Henry Raeburn, the inventions of Watt and the economics of Adam Smith were only part of the picture.

But it was the ideas of philosophers like David Hume and Dugald Stewart that really took hold in the colonies. Here was a nation in the very throes of carving out an identity for itself, and the practical thinking of acclaimed Scots held huge appeal.

Dugald Stewart, along with Thomas Reid and Adam Fergusson, had evolved a very no-nonsense philosophy – the philosophy of Common Sense. It was a potent brew of matter-of-fact ideas, so affecting at the time that it was adopted as the official philosophy of France for the next half a century. And it wasn't hard to see why these ideas appealed to a nation pulling itself up by the boot strings and battling it out with a mighty, untamed continent.

Scots philosophy also helped to ferment the notion of revolution against injustice. Scotland's Thomas Reid wrote that certain moral 'truths' were 'self evident' – a common sense expression that must sound very familiar to all Americans today. From a business point of view, Adam Smith argued vehemently against Britain's restrictions on the colonies, while Adam Fergusson supported the colonists' natural rights. Pushy Scots immigrants may have been disliked by other colonists, but these respected men had stayed at home. Their support of the colonists' cause, combined with the practicality and rationality of their ideas, helped thread this very Scottish philosophy even more tightly into the fabric of blossoming American life.

Perhaps the most influential of all Scottish thinkers in America was John Witherspoon from Haddington, a clergyman, appropriately enough, who eventually became principal of Princeton. Witherspoon had left Scotland because he found the liberalism of the Scottish Enlightenment a darned sight *too* liberal for his religious tastes, but he still preached the Common Sense viewpoint when he reached America. Perhaps he missed home after all.

The historian Garry Wills called Witherspoon 'the most influential teacher in the entire history of American education' and one look at who he taught gives some idea of why Scottish attitudes spread to the point where Common Sense was considered the most influential philosophy in the nation.

Witherspoon's pupils included James Madison, who would become president of the United States, and Aaron Burr who would become vice-president. He also taught 3 supreme court judges, 5 cabinet members, 6 signers of the *Declaration of Independence* (and signed it himself – the only clergyman to do so), 9 delegates to the Constitutional Convention, 12 state governors, 21 US senators, 29 US representatives, 31 army officers who fought on the Revolutionary side, 56 state legislators and over 100 ministers.

Unlike the universities of Harvard and Yale, who had a very local student body, Princeton contained students from all over America. When they graduated, they went back home, spreading Witherspoon's message across the entire country.

Soon after their founding, most of the colonial colleges were using Francis Hutcheson's *System of Moral Philosophy* as a standard textbook. Hutcheson was the son and grandson of Scottish Presbyterian clergymen. King's College (which became Columbia University) even insisted on a two-year study of his work. Benjamin Franklin himself knew all the Scots philosophers, and spent his last night in Scotland with Adam Fergusson, while Thomas Jefferson credited his Scottish tutor, William Small, with having 'probably fixed the destinies of my life'.

One of the most influential figures of the American Revolution was Thomas Paine, whose pamphlet, appropriately called *Common Sense*, sold half a million copies and profoundly affected the thinking of the revolutionaries. What most people don't know is that he attended Adam Fergusson's lectures in London before emigrating to America.

Looking back, there are enormous similarities in the basic structures of the US government and the Scottish Presbyterian Church. Both institutions have tiers of democracy that range upwards from local, through regional to a national level. There have even been historians who claim that the US governmental structure was deliberately copied from the Scottish Presbyterian Church.

The American *Declaration of Independence* is the culmination of the colonist's revolutionary ideas and is famous all over the world for its splendid sentiments, brilliant wording and admirable ideals. The *Encyclopaedia Britannica* states that the *Declaration of Independence* 'contained the first formal assertion by a whole people of their right to a government of their own choice'.

That statement is simply not true. There had been two previous declarations of the same sort and both of them were Scottish, an ironic omission by the *Encyclopaedia Britannica*, considering it, too, had originated in Scotland.

As far back as 1320, the *Declaration of Arbroath* was drafted – an assertion of Scotland's independence from England. Addressed to the Pope, and signed by several dozen representatives, it insisted on the people's right to choose their own government.

Then, in 1638, came the National Covenant, which challenged the King's authority to impose his political and religious will on the people of Scotland. This covenant was copied and carried to 'every burgh, parish and university' in Scotland, and was signed by a huge cross-section of the population.

These documents would have been known to the delegates involved in the drafting of the *Declaration of Independence*. In fact, a comparison of the *Declaration of Independence* and the National Covenant show incredible similarities.

Perhaps the most impressive example of this is in comparing the *Preamble to the Constitution of the United States*, sacred to millions of Americans, to the National Covenant, drafted almost 150 years earlier. Though the *Preamble* is a concise document and the Covenant is undeniably long-winded in comparison, they express exactly the same sentiments and the Covenant, when pared down, contains the same message almost word for word:

PREAMBLE TO THE CONSTITUTION OF THE UNITED STATES (1787)	THE NATIONAL COVENANT AND ACT ORDAINING IT (1638)
We the people of the United States	*We* noblemen, barons, gentlemen, burgesses, ministers and commons considering the great happiness which
in order to form a more *perfect union* *establish justice*	may flow from a full and *perfect union* judiciaries to be *established* and ministration of *justice* among us
ensure domestic tranquillity provide for the *common defence* promote the general welfare	procure true and perfect peace stand to the *mutual defence* for the common happiness to conduce for so good ends and promote the same
and *secure* the blessings of *liberty to ourselves and our posterity* *do ordain* and establish this *constitution* for the United States of America	*security* of said *liberties to ourselves and our posterity* *do ordain* the Covenant and *Constitution* of this Kingdom

The legacy of the Scots lives on in the USA, often unnoticed by its inhabitants. But when the lineage of the 41 past presidents of the United States is examined, an amazing 31 have some form of documented Scots ancestry.

Perhaps the most fitting postscript to this story concerns a man named Samuel Wilson, whose parents had come from Greenock, just outside Glasgow, to live in New York. Wilson ran a food business supplying, among others, the United States Army. Naturally enough, when he shipped beef to the forces, he would stamp 'US' on the barrels. His workers however, with a typical dislike for their Scottish boss, derisively called the barrels 'Uncle Sam's'.

The US troops, knowing nothing of their supplier's real name, assumed that Uncle Sam was new slang for the US government. They adopted the name and the world, unknowingly, went along.

Uncle Sam, though few people realize it, has very Scottish origins indeed.

THE POETS CORNERED AGAIN

Then hurrah! For the mighty monster whale,
Which has got 17 feet 4 inches from tip to tip of a tail!
Which can be seen for sixpence or a shilling
That is to say, if the people all are willing.
WILLIAM McGONAGALL (1825–1902), *THE FAMOUS TAY WHALE*

Scots are justifiably proud of their great poet Robert Burns (1759–96). There is little doubt that he was a formidable talent, as well as one of the most famous poets in the world.

Yet he took a great deal of the influence for his 'unique' style from the lesser known poet Robert Fergusson (1750–74). In the eighteenth century 'Standard Habbie', a form of poetic metre, was popular among Scottish poets. Traditionally used in older satirical verse, Fergusson extended its use to cover more serious subjects, making a great impression on the young Burns. To his credit, Burns freely acknowledged his debt to Fergusson, calling him 'my elder brother in misfortune, but far my elder brother in muse'.

Fergusson was highly regarded in his day and might have given

Burns a run for his money had he not been a manic depressive, dying in Edinburgh's Bedlam Asylum at the age of 24.

There is no denying that Scotland has produced some excellent poets, but, with the exception of Robert Burns and the Bay City Rollers, it hasn't exactly shaken the world in the iambic pentameter department.

Which is a shame, for Scotland has an unknown poetic legacy that no other country in the world can match.

The Scots produced not just one, but the *two* worst poets in the history of the planet.

This is not a claim that can be disputed. They really were that bad.

One was called James McIntyre, born in Forres in 1827. McIntyre emigrated to Canada at the age of 14 but, fortunately for the general population, didn't find his artistic calling for many years. He worked first as a hired hand, then became a furniture dealer and eventually established a furniture factory in Ingersoll, Ontario, the heart of Canada's dairy and cheese-making provinces.

It was in Ingersoll that McIntyre found his vocation, publishing two volumes of collected poems: *Musings on the Banks of the Canadian Thames* and *Poems of James McIntyre*.

At first, McIntyre's poetry covered a variety of topics, albeit badly. Patriotism, Canadian authors, Ontario towns, rural life, foreign wars, poets, philosophers and morality were all grist for his grating poetic mill.

McIntyre's obsession, however, was cheese. He wrote volumes of dairy verse that transcended mere dreadfulness – though it earned him the rather flattering title 'The Chaucer of Cheese'. It's unclear just why he placed cheese above all other subjects – or even above all other dairy products – McIntyre's verse manages to convey something akin to worship.

Take *Ode on the Mammoth Cheese* (*Weight over seven thousand pounds*), for instance.

It honestly has to be read to be believed.

> We have seen thee, queen of cheese,
> Lying quietly at your ease,
> Gently fanned by evening breeze,
> Thy fair form no flies dare seize.
>
> All gaily dressed soon you'll go
> To the great Provincial show,
> To be admired by many a beau
> In the city of Toronto.
>
> Cows numerous as a swarm of bees,
> Or as the leaves upon the trees,
> It did require to make thee please.
> And stand unrivalled, queen of cheese.
>
> May you not receive a scar as
> We have heard that Mr. Harris
> Intends to send you off as far as
> Folks would think it was the moon
> About to fall and crush them soon.

Pretty hard to beat.

But if James McIntyre was abysmal, William Topaz McGonagall took poetry to an all-time record-shattering low.

William McGonagall was born in Edinburgh and grew up with very little schooling, but a great deal of tenacity, both of which were very much in evidence when he started to write. He lived in Dundee, worked most of his life as a weaver and, thankfully, didn't compose a poem until the age of 52. Then he received a 'divine inspiration', as he put it so eloquently in his autobiography.

> It was the year of 1877 and in the month of June, when the flowers were in full bloom. [Even then the poetry was creeping in.] Well, it being the holiday week in Dundee, I was sitting in my back room in Paton's Lane, Dundee, lamenting to myself because I couldn't get to the Highlands on holiday to see the beautiful scenery, when all of a sudden my body got inflamed, and instantly I was seized with a strong desire to write poetry, so strong, in fact, that in my imagination I thought I heard a voice crying in my ears – Write! Write!

And write he did. Giving up his weaving job, he spent the rest of his life composing literary gems – 215 pieces in all, including a play.

But it is for his poetry that William Topaz McGonagall will, quite rightly, go down in history. It is disjointed, doesn't scan and goes off on incredible tangents at the drop of a hat. The rhyme pays no attention whatsoever to the overall narrative and if McGonagall found two words he liked that rhymed, he'd use them over and over – often within the same poem. The extent of the awfulness he could achieve is perfectly encapsulated in a verse from 'The Demon Drink'. McGonagall manages to become completely sidetracked after only one line and still provide the conclusion he was aiming for, by attacking a completely different subject. It is a truly masterful performance.

> The man that gets drunk is little else than a fool,
> And is in the habit, no doubt, of advocating for Home Rule;
> But the best Home Rule for him, as far as I can understand,
> Is the abolition of strong drink from the land.

McGonagall was in fact very popular in Dundee, where he lived most of his life. Crowds would flock to see his recitals, but not to appreciate them. Rather they would treat the whole thing as comic entertainment and fire peas or launch tomatoes at the unfortunate bard.

The 'great poet and tragedian' was convinced of his own genius, however, and once walked 50 miles on foot to try to convince Queen Victoria to be his patron. When he reached the gates of Balmoral he was told to go away and never come back.

He went to London, lured by forged invitations (McGonagall was the butt of countless practical jokes which he never got, even after they had been revealed to him) and even travelled to New York, arriving with only eight shillings. The Americans didn't like his poetry any better than the Scots and he quickly came back.

McGonagall has the last laugh, in a way. Everything he ever wrote has been published, and he is still read avidly today by a core of loyal admirers. Just as Shakespeare, his idol, is regarded as the greatest literary writer in history – McGonagall is seen, without doubt, as the worst. As such, he is equally deserving of his place in history.

It is hard to know how to take William McGonagall. He is perfect for ridiculing and great fun for any country to claim as its own. The Scots can boast about him, and in doing so show that they can laugh at themselves.

Yet McGonagall's attempts to express himself were not funny to him. And the treatment he received from his own countrymen was lamentable, when all he wanted was to better himself through his love of performance and poetry. William Power in *My Scotland* gives this account of a show that the ageing McGonagall gave in Glasgow.

> After reciting some of his own poems, to an accompaniment of whistles and cat calls, the Bard armed himself with a most dangerous-looking broadsword, and strode up and down the platform, declaiming 'Clarence's Dream' and 'Give me another horse – bind up my wounds'. His voice rose to a howl. He thrust and slashed at imaginary foes. A shower of apples and oranges fell on the platform. Almost before they touched it, they were met by the fell edge of McGonagall's claymore and cut to pieces. The Bard was beaded with perspiration and orange juice. The audience yelled with delight. McGonagall yelled louder still, with a fury which I fancy was not wholly feigned. It was like a squalid travesty of the wildest scenes of *Don Quixote* and *Orlando Furioso*. I left the hall early, saddened and disgusted.

The comparison with Don Quixote is apt. McGonagall has become a figure of ridicule, but his bravado was more than admirable. He may have been the world's worst poet, but he didn't let that stand in his way. He had an impossible dream and he went for it.

There is a lesson to be learned from this. One can condemn Fergusson's economy or scoff at McIntyre or McGonagall's awful verse.

Or one can admire their, typically Scottish, drive.

THE ORIGIN OF
THE ORIGIN OF SPECIES

I have forgot a great deal more than most other men know.

JAMES BURNETT (LORD MONBODDO)

Man is not a divine creation but is descended, instead, from lower life forms. This idea rocked the foundations of society and threw established religion into a frenzy. Nobody wanted to be a monkey's uncle.

The credit for the theory of evolution has gone to the naturalist Charles Darwin, but this is a little misleading. The theory, like its subject matter, was a process of natural evolution: Darwin was only one of a number of scientists circling this groundbreaking but controversial idea. Darwin was influenced and encouraged by the likes of Thomas Huxley and the Scotsman Sir Charles Lyell and in 1858, to his astonishment, received a memoir from the explorer, Alfred Russell Wallace, containing the main ideas of his own theory of natural selection. Charles Lyell and Joseph Hooker persuaded Darwin to quickly submit a paper of his own, which was read, along with Wallace's, before the Linnean Society.

The Origin of Species by Means of Natural Selection, published in 1859, is an epoch-making book and there is no question about the magnitude of Darwin's achievement. But he wasn't the only one playing around with such subversive ideas – the fact that Alfred Wallace beat him to a finished written theory (and coined the phrase 'natural selection') is proof of that.

Yet, once again, there was an unknown Scotsman delving into these ideas before anyone else. Almost a hundred years before Darwin, an Edinburgh judge came up with a theory of evolution, and influenced the great naturalist in a way that nobody could have imagined.

His name was Lord Monboddo.

Lord Monboddo (1714–99) was born James Burnett at Monboddo, Kincardine in 1714. He was educated at King's College in Aberdeen, but narrow-minded tutoring in his youth gave him a rather odd quirk. He developed a passion for all things classical which bordered on the obsessive. As a young man he settled in Edinburgh and, in 1737, was admitted as a member of the Faculty of Advocates, working his way up to become one of the most eminent judges at the Court of Session.

Unfortunately, Monboddo is remembered more for his rampant eccentricity than anything else. His love of classical culture led him to scorn modern mores. Though it was all the rage in Edinburgh to travel in sedan chairs, the Greeks and Romans didn't do it, so neither would Monboddo. He chose to ride on horseback, no matter how nasty the weather, but did deign to put his powdered wig in a sedan chair if it rained.

These peculiarities made Monboddo the target of endless jibes, and anecdotes about his legendary dottiness persist to this day. In 1778, for instance, Monboddo was visiting the King's Court in London, when there was an alarm about the safety of the ceiling. The entire chamber rushed outside with the exception of Monboddo, who sat where he was until the all-clear was given and everyone trooped sheepishly back inside. When asked why he had not evacuated with the others, Monboddo explained he thought it was 'an annual ceremony, with which, as an alien, he had nothing to do'.

Though the story is true, it must be remembered that Monboddo was 71 years old by this time. He was also deaf and partially blind and had suffered a serious illness that impaired his mental abilities. It's a testament to the man's strength of will that he made it to London in the first place.

The main focus for local derision, however, was Monboddo's belief that orang-utans were capable of speech and that parts of the world held humans with tails. Monboddo had translated these 'facts' from a manuscript by a Swedish sailor named Koeping who had written an account of his world travels. The stories describe several zoological and botanical oddities, including the unlikely fact that the Nicobar islanders had tails. Though disinclined, at first, to believe Koeping's far-fetched observations, Monboddo finally admitted, 'He writes in a simple plain manner, not like a man who intended to impose a lie upon the world, merely for the silly pleasure of making people stare.'

Monboddo had the kind of mind which could easily accept that astonishing things might be true, and it opened him up to all sorts of ridicule. Had Koeping written reports of dinosaur bones or pygmy tribes, Monboddo's acceptance of them would have been treated with equally derisive glee.

The judge's apparent weirdness overshadowed his philosophical musings, including an idea that made men with tails look positively conservative.

Monboddo eventually concluded that human beings were products of evolution.

The idea came about during the writing of the judge's epic tome *Of The Origin and Progress of Language*. This long-winded book runs into several volumes and Monboddo added to it constantly: it takes enthusiasm bordering on the obsessive to trawl through the whole thing.

At that time, many respected writers tackled the subject of language, including Adam Smith, Thomas Reid and Lord Kames. Yet only Monboddo bothered with the abandoned Aristotelian notion that language was not necessarily a gift from God – that it might have been acquired through a process of evolution. Taken from that perspective, a book about the origins of language was a philosophically loaded gun. Monboddo himself was aware of the path he had committed himself to taking, setting out what he intended to prove:

> First, that language is not Natural to Man – second, that it is
> possible (for I say no more) that it may have been invented –
> and, lastly – upon that Supposition – to show how it was
> invented.

This is quite a leap from the established notion that God provided man
with the dubious gift of conversation. It also vilifies Monboddo's odd
beliefs about orang-utans. In a way they *are* capable of speech – today
some apes have been taught rudimentary sign language. According to
the prevailing theories of the day, apes were not capable of speech,
because they lacked the divine gift of a rational soul, an objection
voiced to Monboddo by his friend Lord Lyttelton. In Monboddo's eyes,
apes were only incapable of speech because they hadn't developed the
physical and mental skills to communicate.

Who looks more eccentric now?

From this controversial stance, however, Monboddo moved into even
more dangerous territory:

> Man is formed, not however all at once, but by degrees, and in
> succession: for he appears at first to be little more than a
> vegetable, hardly deserving the name of Zoophyte; then he
> gets sense [sensitivity to pain], but sense only so that he is yet
> little better than a muscle [mollusc]; then he becomes an
> animal of a more complete kind; then a rational creature, and
> finally a man of intellect and science.

He went on to argue that the modern humans originated somewhere
warm like Egypt and then spread over the rest of the globe and learned
to use simple tools and to band together in defensive units, at this point
becoming equal to the great apes. Then humankind began to form
tribes with a rough form of social regulation and the beginnings of
speech. As society developed, language improved and physical prowess
declined, leading to the evolution of the modern human we see today.

It all sounds very familiar.

Monboddo also saw the dangers inherent in this 'acquired'
civilisation. He saw that the development of language and intellect
would bring art and science – and that some of these arts and sciences
would have the power to degrade the human race as well as to uplift it.
As a result, Monboddo believed that the human race would ultimately
bring about its own destruction.

If Monboddo's belief in men with tails caused derision, his examination of human origins and where we were all headed caused apoplexy. But in the twentieth century, his theory is more or less accepted and his warning voiced by more and more people.

Monboddo may have bordered on the insane but he also had his fair share of genius.

This is not to say that the good judge wasn't way off base about a lot of things – today only a masochist would plough through Monboddo's two very long epics, *The Origin and Progress of Language* and *Ancient Metaphysics*. Monboddo suffered from a ponderous literary style, a scattergun approach to his subjects and the inability to know when to stop writing. In addition, he was no scientist and he knew it – Monboddo's theories stemmed from intellectual inspiration, not scientific study.

It was a struggle that sometimes proved too great for him. His open-minded view of human origins was at odds with his belief in God and his love of the classics. Especially distressing to him were the more modern writings of Newton and Locke. Monboddo didn't have the mathematical ability to match Newton, and Locke's mechanistic implications for the human race horrified the ageing judge.

As the years wore on, Monboddo's eccentricities grew more pronounced and were not helped by the sudden death of his beloved daughter Eliza and his own near-fatal illness.

Yet Lord Neaves, one of Monboddo's successors on the bench, had little doubt about the legal giant's influence on the theory of evolution:

> Though Darwin now proclaims the law
> And spreads it far abroad, O!
> The man that first the secret saw
> Was honest old Monboddo
> The architect precedence takes
> Of him that bears the hod, O!
> So up and at them, Land of Cakes,
> We'll vindicate Monboddo.

An excruciating poem, certainly – but to the point.

Did Charles Darwin know of Monboddo's work? He certainly never mentioned him – though his famous grandfather, Erasmus, refers to the judge in his book *The Temple of Nature*.

Darwin did, however, study medicine at Edinburgh University. He found most of the lectures dull and the subject of anatomy 'disgusting', and left after two years. But for those two years he studied a hundred yards from the picturesque Greyfriars Cemetery – the burial place of Lord Monboddo.

There is little doubt that Darwin heard the stories of the eccentric judge and his oddball theories. And one, certainly, seems to have stuck in his mind.

After all, that's how natural selection works.

GREAT SCOTT

Oh what a tangled web we weave,
When first we practise to deceive.
SIR WALTER SCOTT, *MARMION*

The Scottish and English crowns were joined in 1605, to the great rejoicing of most of the Scots, who thought they had gained some kind of victory. A century later, in 1707, the two countries parliaments united and, this time, the Scots were not so happy. They suspected their independence was slowly slipping away.

They were right. A century later, the highlanders had been crushed and the north of Scotland systematically emptied. The Lowland Scots' autonomy was eradicated in a more peaceful, but no less effective, manner. Joined to the larger and more prosperous England by crown, politics and law, the lowlander gradually lost his identity to English manners, fashion and lifestyle.

In an attempt to retain traditional Scottish customs, language and dress evolved into something quite ludicrous. The idle rich of Scotland formed Celtic clubs like the Society of the True Highlander, a mere pretence at keeping ancient Scottish culture alive. For a start, membership was limited to those of 'property and birth', which effectively prevented real highlanders from joining. The aim of clubs like the Society of the True Highlander was to let men of property and birth hang out with each other and hunt and fish on land where the Celts used to roam free.

The common Scot didn't much care any more for the trappings of national identity; preoccupied instead with getting doing a job and taking what frugal pleasures were available from the hard life of a worker. Whether he or she was Scottish or English didn't much alter the day-to-day realities of existence.

But a chain of events building in the corridors of English power would forever change how Scotland saw itself – and alter the world's perception of this little country.

And one Scotsman became the catalyst for this incredible change: Sir Walter Scott.

In England, King George IV was not popular. He was portly, sick, ageing, out of touch with his people and involved in a messy public divorce. He had also expressed a desire to attend the Congress of Nations in Vienna. The English government was horrified by this idea – George was not exactly a people person and was fairly clueless about affairs of state. To keep him from meddling in international power-broking, his ministers came up with a much safer alternative – they organised a trip to Scotland instead. After all, there hadn't been an official visit by a British monarch to Scotland for 200 years. The north might conceivably be pleased to see him.

Considering how unpopular George was in England, this didn't sound like such a bad idea. Once he got used to the notion that he was going to rainy Scotland rather than influential Vienna, the ageing monarch threw himself into the enterprise with gusto. Knowing nothing of the animosity between the Lowlands where he'd actually be staying, and the Highlands, the king decided that wearing Highland dress would be appropriate. Having no real idea what normal Highland dress looked like, he got George Hunter & Company of London to design him a costume, paying an amount for it that most highlanders could have lived on for several years.

The finished mockery was made of satin, velvet and cashmere in eye-popping scarlet weave – now sold all over Scotland as the Royal Stuart Tartan – and the whole outfit was adorned with more brooches, precious metals and jewels than would be found in the average Egyptian tomb. It was an affront to the simple belted plaid worn by the real highlander, but in true 'Emperor's New Clothes' tradition, nobody was going to point that out to the King.

Up north, the Scots were equally excited about the first visit by a monarch in two centuries, blissfully unaware that they were George's second choice for a holiday destination. The Scottish gentry wanted to make everything perfect for this great honour, and there was only one man thought equal to the task of organising such an immense event – Sir Walter Scott, the novelist.

Scott was an immensely influential and charismatic figure, and by far the most famous man in the country. Not only had he written highly popular (and highly romanticised) novels about the glorious Highlands, but he had also managed quite an amazing national coup. He had 'found' the honours of Scotland – the Scottish Crown Jewels.

The fact that they had been lost in the first place is a measure of how low Scottish national esteem had dropped. In fact, the honours had lain, wrapped in rags, in a chest in Edinburgh Castle for generations, until Scott suggested to George that they should be restored to their former glory. When the chest was opened Scott was the first one to peer in, with bated breath, and see that the forgotten crown jewels were still intact. That they are now on display in Edinburgh Castle is thanks, largely, to him.

If anyone was going to whip up Scottish national fervour for a foreign king ruling from England, Walter Scott was the man to do it.

Scott had a truly astounding talent for myth-making. His writings about America, for instance, prompted a blistering attack from Mark Twain, who more or less accused Scott of starting the American Civil War.

> It was Sir Walter that made every gentlemen in the South a Major or a Colonel, or a General or a Judge, before the war; and it was he, also, that made these gentlemen value these bogus decorations. For it was he that created rank and caste, and pride and pleasure in them. Enough is laid on slavery, without fathering upon it these creations and contributions of Sir Walter.
>
> Sir Walter had so large a hand in making Southern character, as it existed before the war, that he is in great measure responsible for the war.

Nominated as Scotland's official representative, Walter Scott set out to make George's visit as memorable as possible.

He had no idea just how memorable 'the king's jaunt' would actually become.

Scott put together a committee to organise events, but they were little more than implementers of his own grand vision and the novelist worked himself to exhaustion trying to oversee every detail of the whole affair.

Scott's romantic vision of the royal trip was a natural extension of his writing. His theme was clearly set out. 'When His Majesty comes amongst us,' Scott wrote, 'he comes to his ancient kingdom of Scotland, and must be received according to ancient usages.'

Figuring out what those 'ancient usages' actually might be was the problem. Scots myths, partly invented by the novelist, were now mixed freely with historical reality, and few could distinguish one from the other.

Thanks to Walter Scott's boundless enthusiasm and fervent imagination, what eventually occurred was an extravagant, never to be forgotten, pantomime. The Scots played at being what an absentee English king expected them to be, and hammed up every aspect of that performance, right down to the exaggerated costumes.

In an attempt to give suitable depth to the proceedings, Scott leapt at any chance to mythologise. The Company of Archers, for instance, suddenly found that they were the 'ancient bodyguards of the kings of Scotland', which was news to them. Before that, the Archers had been little more than a gentleman's club. Scott's evocation was, naturally, more to their taste and the Archers happily went along with it – a myth that persists to this day. In the spirit of the occasion, the Company of Archers turned up for the king's visit sporting tight-fitting Lincoln green and white satin. Nobody blinked an eye.

It became obvious that Scottish garb of some variety was going to be the order of the day and now everyone wanted in on the act. Fortunately most people were not as flamboyant, or as tasteless, as the Archers. In fact, the general population weren't sure just *what* to wear. Scots didn't really have a national dress that could be identified as their own, especially not in the Lowlands. Highlanders wore simple belted plaids, but these were far too practical and drab for such a special occasion. Besides, nobody in the south of Scotland liked them.

The Lowland Scots wanted a proper uniform. Something that would immediately identify them as true Scotsmen to this visiting dignitary –

and they looked to Walter Scott for the answer. The novelist dashed out a quick booklet entitled *Hints addressed to the Inhabitants of Edinburgh and others in Prospect of His Majesty's Visit*. Scott did not add his name to the pamphlet, but everyone knew it to be his work. In this quickly written propaganda piece, Scott pointed out that, since George IV was descended (tentatively) from the House of Stuart, most notable Scots families could claim kinship with him. The ordinary Scot-in-the-street was likened to one great clan with the king as their chief. In a passage reminiscent of promises made by the US government to American Indians, Scott exhorted the people of Edinburgh to treat George as if he were a 'father' to their people.

He neglected to mention that George was the great-nephew of the Duke of Cumberland, who had butchered the highlanders after Culloden.

The booklet also told the average worker, gentleman and lady exactly what was appropriate dress for the state visit. Ladies, for instance, were to wear at least nine feathers in every headdress. Scott wasn't exactly *au fait* with ladies' fashion and English gentlewomen gawped in astonishment at the bobbing, overburdened heads of their Scots counterparts.

The *Scotsman* newspaper was bold enough to suggest that perhaps the king ought to see his subjects in their normal clothes, but it was too late – everybody loves to dress up for an occasion, and this was the greatest occasion in living memory.

Besides, nobody was getting as togged-up as the king himself. The highlight of the state visit was to be a Grand Ball at the Edinburgh Assembly Rooms, where the king, Scott declared, would be wearing 'a magnificent dress of the Royal Tartan'. It was only natural, then, that the ball should have a similar dress code: 'No Gentleman is to be allowed to appear in any thing but the ancient Highland costume'.

There was nothing else for it. If the king was going to sport Highland dress, then everyone else would have to. Gentlemen who would normally run a mile rather than put on a kilt, plaid or trews were not going to miss out on the party of a lifetime because they didn't have the right outfit. Perhaps acting out the role of an ancient Highland warrior wouldn't be too bad if they could spruce up that dull northern garb to their own specifications. The gentry set about designing their own brightly coloured tartan costumes with gusto.

Which left one last problem. The king expected to see some real highlanders on his visit – not just a bunch of southerners running about in newly made kilts. Since George had no intention of going near the

Highlands, Walter Scott sent out a call inviting northern clan chiefs to Edinburgh. The novelist's reputation ensured that his request was not treated lightly. After all, Scott's writing had painted the clans in glowing colours – they owed him one.

Besides, many clan chiefs of 1822 bore no resemblance to their warlike predecessors. Instead, they were gentlemen with acquired gentrified manners and a fondness for the good life down south. They were positively eager to attend.

The problem was, what to wear for this magnificent occasion? Highland dress, whatever it might be, had been banned for 80 years. The snooty Highland societies dedicated to 'preserving' Celtic traditions certainly couldn't provide realistic guidelines. Alaisdair Ranaldson MacDonnell, Fifteenth Chief of Glengarry, summed up the absurdity of adopting costumes 'preserved' by these self-congratulatory societies in his description of the Celtic Society of Edinburgh:

> I dined one day with them since, and I never saw so much tartan before in my life, with so little Highland material . . . they have no right to burlesque the national character or dress of Highlands, against the continuance of which, so mortifying to the feelings of all real highlanders, I, for one, formally protest.

The highlanders were willing enough to take part in this great Scottish pageant. They realised this was a great occasion and didn't want to appear shoddy, but they were rough-living folk with clothes to match. The chiefs were even more concerned. Some northern landowners were being fiercely criticised for the treatment of their own clans: accused of clearing their own people from the land and mistreating those who stayed. Turning up with a bunch of bedraggled, colourless minions would simply reinforce that image.

They needed to put on a display as much as the king wanted to see it.

Once again, Scott came to the rescue. At his suggestion, chiefs like Sir Evan Murray Macgregor ordered new tartan costumes wholesale from weaving firms like John Callander and Company and the Wilson Brothers of Bannockburn. These firms were already making tartans for the army and had no problem in conjuring up a 'traditional' clan tartan whenever the occasion required.

Decked out in their new, mass-manufactured 'outfits', the highlanders exhibited enough sartorial approval to be allowed to parade in front of their Hanoverian king – the dynasty that had ordered the annihilation of their grandfathers.

By the time George IV actually arrived, anticipation had built into a frenzy. So great was the demand for tartan outfits that, in one week, three hundred unemployed tailors were hired in Edinburgh alone.

When George IV finally did set foot on Scotland's shore, he was something of a letdown. He was a portly and unglamorous man, and his penchant for stuffing himself into military style outfits and tartan apparel didn't help.

Still, the elaborate and unflattering costumes he wore at the beginning of his visit were positively conservative compared to his outfit for the Grand Ball at the Edinburgh Assembly Rooms. His appearance caused a mixture of shock, outrage and admiration at the sheer audacity of his get-up. His large body was crammed into a bright red tartan plaid and velvet jacket dripping with jewellery – and a pair of flesh coloured hose encased his portly legs. Even the most dandified gentry were taken aback.

Scott had put on such a magnificent show that the least impressive aspect of it was poor old George IV himself.

It didn't matter. In the end, the king's visit was far more important to Scotland than it was to the king.

Walter Scott had done more than put on a pageant. He had altered a nation's perception of itself. The highlanders, looking splendid in their new clothes, had paraded through the very heart of the Lowlands without any animosity aroused on either side. They found to their amazement that the lowlanders seemed proud of them, rather than suspicious and vengeful. The lowlanders, on the other hand, found they were no longer afraid of these highlanders, who (not surprisingly in the contrived circumstances) looked far more romantic than they had ever imagined. In August 1822, for the first time in its history, Scotland was an undivided nation. And for the first time, the Scots had a national uniform to go along with their newly acquired solidarity.

Lady Stafford, in a letter to Walter Scott, expressed her hope for Scotland's future: a hope echoed by the whole population:

> I rejoice to think that this visit of the King's to Scotland, that
> as it has been will do a great deal to excite the [conscience] of
> the country in every way & to bring the Highlanders forward,

who have not been overlooked on this occasion, & we shall all
revive our tartans & our badges & our national manners &
language with increased satisfaction.

In many ways the 'jaunt' of 1822 has never ended. The elaborate dress,
the multiple tartans, the blending of Highland and Lowland identity –
these images adorn a million postcards, gift-shop windows and
shortbread tins. They *are* Scotland.

Walter Scott exceeded his wildest dreams. His tartan pageant had
made his romantic, absurd and totally manufactured vision of Scotland
a reality – and one that has grown stronger with each passing year. As
the historian John Prebble so accurately put it, 'No other nation has
cherished so absurd an image, and none perhaps would accept it while
knowing it to be a lie.'

Yet, in a way, it was a wonderful lie. It gave Scotland back its pride.
A country that had lost its monarch, then its independence, then its
very identity suddenly saw itself as a nation again.

And a nation based on one man's invention is better than no nation
at all.

SOLDIER BLUES

They are hardy, intrepid, accustomed to a rough country, and no great mischief if they fall.

GENERAL JAMES WOLFE (1727–59), TALKING OF HIGHLAND SOLDIERS

In the last hundred years, the Campbells of Cawdor, a relatively small branch of Clan Campbell, have been awarded 12 mentions in dispatches, 3 brevets, 3 French Croix de Guerre (one with palm and star), 4 Legions of Honour, 3 Victoria Crosses and 20 other medals.

The bravery of the Scots soldier is legendary. Yet the Scottish armies rarely won battles and never won a war. Hampered by inferior weapons, unclear goals and lack of military training, the Scots may have been keen to rumble, but they almost always came off worst.

There were other reasons for the Scots' poor military history. Too much aggression, rather than lack of it, was a detrimental factor – the Scots rarely fought on one side when they could fight on both. Highlanders fought against lowlanders. Highlanders fought against highlanders. Lowlanders fought against borderers. Catholics fought against Protestants.

It's pretty hard to win a battle when you're always up against your own people.

When they weren't fighting each other, the Scots conflicts were always against their old adversary, the English. The bravery of the common soldier in these skirmishes was beyond question, but the leadership skills of their commanders were questionable at best. Few Scots leaders gave proper thought to tactics – like the inadvisability of tackling larger and better-equipped armies head on. Even when the Scots had numerical superiority, their own enthusiasm was often their undoing. The warriors were so anxious to get into the fight that they'd abandon superior positions in their haste to reach the enemy. Either their leaders couldn't prevent this from happening, or they actually joined in.

The Battle of Flodden is a perfect example. In 1513, at the request of his French allies, James IV led the greatest Scots army of all time into England. Helpfully, he sent his best artillerymen to France before marching south to Flodden. Though James had the better defensive position, larger cannon and five times as many men, the English had artillerymen who actually knew what they were doing. The ensuing bombardment persuaded the Scots to leave their higher position and attack.

Scots spearmen charged down the hill, having taken off their shoes to get a better grip on the slippery ground. They were armed with the traditional 16-foot pike, but the English had a new weapon, the halberd, a combination of spear and axe. One chop with a halberd and the Scots found their 16-foot pikes were 8-foot pikes. Then 4-foot pikes. Eventually they were fighting with toothpicks.

James IV, leading the centre battalion, actually fought to within a spear's length of the English commander before he was killed. Flodden wasn't so much a defeat as utter annihilation.

Lack of success in battle, however, never deterred the Scots from having a go. In the north, the highlander's tribal lifestyle virtually demanded it. If there wasn't a decent war going on at home, they would rent themselves out to other countries as mercenaries.

Scots fighters fared much better abroad than they did in their own country. In other lands they had the benefit of foreign experience, money, equipment and discipline. Combined with the Scots hardiness and natural aggression, these elements turned the Caledonian mercenaries into formidable forces.

Lifting the siege of Orleans in 1429, Joan of Arc entered the city under a Scottish designed flag, marching to the Scots tune *L'Air des Soldats De Robert Bruce*, and conducted by 500 Scots soldiers commanded by Patrick Ogilvy.

The Scotsman Bernard Stuart captured Genoa and conquered Lombardy for the French in 1499 and, in 1570, the Scots Brigade played a major role in helping the Dutch throw off Spanish oppression.

In the seventeenth century, Sweden of all countries, became the major military power in Europe. At that time a major proportion of the Swedish army – as many as 40,000 – were Scots. So were a huge number of their military commanders, including Alexander Leslie who commanded the entire Swedish army.

In Scotland, the home team rarely scored so highly. With notable exceptions like Robert the Bruce and the Marquis of Montrose, Scots leaders were either too self-seeking or gung-ho to achieve victory: Earl Hague, Commander in Chief of the British forces during World War I, is the ultimate example of that.

The Scots got their warlike reputation not by being victorious in confrontations, but by the sheer bravado of their doomed enterprises and an audacity that some might call stupidity. Though the Lowland Scots could fight every bit as fiercely, it was the highlander who came to personify the suicidal bravado that substituted for actually winning. The Jacobite uprisings in the Highlands never stood a chance, but the highlanders fought anyway – it was what they did. In fact, they were so keen, some of them fought on both sides.

The best, and saddest, example of this ill-fated courage was the Battle of Culloden. Charles Edward Stuart and 4,000 highlanders faced 9,000 seasoned government troops led by the Duke of Cumberland. Against the advice of his more experienced generals, the 'Bonnie Prince' chose the flat landscape of Culloden Moor for the battle – a perfect spot for government artillery to wreak havoc.

Under withering cannon fire, Charles was forced to give the order to charge, exactly as Cumberland had anticipated. Battered, starved and exhausted, the prince's army went into battle as if they were fresh troops – for all the good it did them. As the Jacobites came hurtling towards them, a gale blowing in their faces, the Redcoats poured volley after volley into them. Incredibly, some Scots actually reached the enemy but the Redcoats simply had too many troops to lose. In half an hour it was all over.

In legend and in song Culloden is lamented as the highlander's last stand against English might. But Culloden certainly wasn't a battle of

Scots against English. There were highlanders and lowlanders on both sides.

As always, the Scots were their own worst enemies.

It is one of the great ironies of history that the Scottish soldier didn't become successful until he joined forces with his greatest enemy. After a thousand years of being defeated in battle, Scots stopped fighting for themselves and were recruited by the British Army. It was only then that they achieved victory after victory.

The British Army trained and equipped the northern warriors and forced on them the one thing they had always lacked – discipline. Within a remarkably short period, the shambolic, violent Scottish rabble had turned into one of the finest fighting forces of all time, the backbone of an army that carved out the greatest empire the world has ever seen.

Scots armies had always consisted of ordinary men who banded together every time their king, noble or chief wanted a war. As part of the British Army, Scots were now actually soldiers, a real profession, and they finally turned their famed ingenuity and enterprise to the field, instead of just turning up to fight.

In 1805, a Scottish clergyman called Alexander John Forsythe invented the percussion lock for firearms and designed the basis for the modern cartridge. In terms of firearm development, this innovation stands second only to gunpowder itself. William Malcolm invented telescopic sights and James Lee, of the legendary Lee-Enfield rifle, was born in Scotland. Scots also invented the smokescreen, the carronade (a type of cannon), the aircraft carrier, cordite, radar and the gas mask, perfected the science of ballistics and tested the first shrapnel.

Champions of the run-right-at-them-and-knock-them-down school of combat, the Scots now found they were remarkably adept at subterfuge. It was an aspect of war that suited their secretive yet entrepreneurial nature. Colonel R. Macleod commanded project Skye, the massive, covert World War II operation that convinced the Germans a huge British 'Fourth Army' was massing in Scotland for an overseas attack. This tied up enough German troops and equipment to allow the real Allied invasion to take place in Normandy. Britain's élite, enigmatic fighting group, the SAS – founded by Lt Col David Stirling and General Colin Gubbins from the Hebrides – commanded the network of spies and saboteurs who operated behind German lines before D-Day.

Even today the British foreign office employs an unusually high percentage of Scots, both in the diplomatic service and the secret service. In the spy novel *Smiley's People*, John Le Carré's hero wonders, 'Why . . . are Scots so attracted to the secret world? Ships' engineers, colonial administrators, spies.'

The most famous example is also drawn from literature: James Bond, 007, is a Scotsman – as was Alexander Fleming, his creator.

But, despite these interesting creative outlets, the pure fighting spirit of the Scots soldier was always his real strength. The Scots foot soldiers, especially the highlanders, were famed for their loyalty in battle as much as their bravery – they would not back down in front of their chief. As the Secretary at War, Lord Barrington, told Parliament in 1751:

> I am for having always in our army as many Scottish soldiers as possible; not that I think them more brave than those of any other country we can recruit from, but because they are generally more hardy and less mutinous.

The British Army exploited this loyalty mercilessly. After all, the Highland troops were originally recruited by the government to be used as cannon fodder, the perfect solution to quell Scotland's rebellious nature. As members of the British forces, highlanders could be sent far away from their own country and placed in the front line. If they won, fine. If they were killed, that was fine too – it meant less Scots to come home and cause trouble again.

It's no real surprise that the Scots quickly acquired the reputation of always being in the thick of the fighting. That's where the British Army always put them. It was a great way to acquire a military reputation, but disastrous in terms of casualty figures – the old Scots armies may not have won very often, but they also reserved the option to run away if they felt they were going to get wiped out.

The authority imposed on the Scots soldier by the British Army eventually turned into a genuine sense of pride in their own achievements. The Scots were finally winning, and now no price was too high to pay, no matter who they fought for. The American Army, for instance, recruited few Scottish immigrants or even Scottish descendants, but awarded its highest honour, the congressional Medal of Honour, to no fewer than 38 soldiers born in Scotland.

In a sense the Scots warrior had come full circle. Once again, he fought on the front line with a bravery that verged on suicidal and suffered tremendous losses. The only difference was that now he was usually on the winning side.

The Scots have paid a terrible price for their reputation. During the First World War 20 per cent of everyone killed from Britain were Scots, even though they made up less than 10 per cent of the total population.

A nation can only lose so many of its youngest, strongest men without paying the price. Some would say it is obvious now that Scotland has paid a high price indeed.

In military terms, it's the misfortune of the Scots that they never had it all. When they ruled themselves they did not have the discipline and leadership – or even the inclination – to fight as a unit. They only became a force to be reckoned with by joining an army that was already a force to be reckoned with, a perfect case of: if you can't beat 'em, join 'em.

This irony is exemplified by the Scots soldier, Patrick Ferguson, who patented the breech-loading rifle, first used against the Americans at the Battle of Brandywine during the War of Independence. In the heat of battle he refused to use his considerable skill as a marksman to shoot an American officer in the back. His newly acquired British stiff upper lip would not allow it.

The officer turned out to be George Washington.

The Scots warrior of old would never have made that mistake.

THE EDISON CON

The first man who thoroughly believed in the possibility and utility of
long-distance wireless telegraphy.
GUGLIELMO MARCONI, WRITING ABOUT JAMES BOWMAN LINDSAY

In 1879, in Menlo Park, New Jersey, Thomas Edison gave a
demonstration of an electric lighting system and the world changed
forever. At one time, whenever night fell, man was afraid to stray
from the flickering fires that held back whatever prowled in the dark.
The candle was a small improvement, the oil lamp more so – at least
people could take a bit of light into the night without the first decent
gust of wind blowing it out.

In time, gas lighting (invented by Scotsman William Murdoch)
allowed cities to have a nightlife of sorts, so long as nobody strayed off
the main street. But it was the electric light that gave man eternal day.
And its invention guaranteed Thomas Alva Edison his place in the
history books.

Edison was an amazing man and thoroughly deserved his fame. He
amassed an astounding 1,098 patents, including the stock ticker, the

mimeograph and the phonograph. However, there is pretty compelling evidence that the most famous achievement by 'The Wizard of Menlo Park' – the invention of the electric light – shouldn't be on his long list of firsts. Champions of the scientist Joseph Swan claim that *he* earned the title 'Father of the Electric Light' by patenting a carbon incandescent lamp nine years earlier. In actual fact, both men were beaten to the title by a mile.

The electric light seems to have been invented by a humble teacher from Dundee named James Bowman Lindsay. Not only did Lindsay produce the world's first electric lighting, he did so an astonishing *40 years* before Edison's patent.

To this day, Lindsay remains an elusive figure. As a man, he was modest, generous and unassuming, passing up chances of fame and fortune in favour of his all-consuming research. A scientist and thinker, he was so immersed in his many projects that he did not feel the need to capitalise on one of the most important inventions in human history.

James Bowman Lindsay was born in the village of Carmylie near Arbroath, on 8 September 1799. His parents were humble farm workers, but Lindsay suffered from ill health as a child and was spared the backbreaking life of a farmhand. Instead, his parents apprenticed him as a handloom linen weaver. When transporting cloth from Carmylie to Arbroath, he would tie the roll onto his shoulders, so that he could read books while walking.

The cloth-weaving son of farm workers was not the ideal candidate to become a literary and scientific giant, but Lindsay's appetite for knowledge was so unstoppable that his parents took a chance and sent him to university.

After a lifetime of self-education, he enrolled in 1821 as a student of St Andrews University in Fife. A diligent worker, he made a name for himself in the fields of mathematics and physics but also completed an additional course in theology. In 1829 he triumphantly moved to Dundee to take up the post of Lecturer in Science and Mathematics at the James Watt institution. But Lindsay's passion for religion and theology had not abated and, in the end, this is what probably doomed him to obscurity.

In the nineteenth century, Dundee had become known as the 'City of Discovery'. A spirit of innovation was gripping the city, resulting in a range of scientific and cultural advances, from the invention of the fixed-focus pocket camera to the first fish and chip shop.

In this bustling metropolis, Lindsay got into his stride. He organised courses on frictional, galvanic and voltaic electricity as well as giving lectures on magnetism and electro-magnetism.

In 1832 he demonstrated the electric telegraph in his classroom and in 1835 made an incredible leap, demonstrating constant electric light, eventually giving a public demonstration at the Thistle Hall in Dundee.

A reporter sent to cover the event wrote in the *Dundee Courier* the next day:

> Mr Lindsay, a teacher in town, succeeded on the evening of Saturday, July 25th in obtaining a constant electric light . . . The light in beauty, surpasses all others, has no smell, emits no smoke, is incapable of explosion and, not requiring air for combustion, can be kept in sealed glass jars . . . it can be sent to any convenient distance and the apparatus for producing it can be contained in a common chest.

The reporter was obviously impressed, though probably not entirely sure of what he was looking at. Lindsay himself wrote a letter to the newspaper about the event, which described the effects of his invention but didn't include the technical details of how it worked – not surprising, considering that public knowledge of electricity was virtually nil.

> I am writing this letter by means of a light at six inches or eight inches distant; and at the present moment can read a book at the distance of one and a half feet. From the same apparatus I can get two or three lights, each of which is fit for reading with. I can make it burn in the open air or in a glass tube without air and neither wind nor water is capable of extinguishing it.

Lindsay prophesied that this miraculous new force, electricity, could be used to light and heat homes as well as drive machinery in industry and, at this point, he seemed poised to enter the world stage as its scientific innovator. But astonishingly, he did not take his research any further. Instead, he stated in a lecture:

> It was in 1830 or 1831 that I turned my particular attention to electricity and I then formed an idea of applying it to mechanical power, illumination and telegraphic com-

> munication . . . I obtained a constant electric light in 1835 and
> devoted a year or two to bring it to perfection.

That was it.

In Lindsay's mind, he had done what he set out to do and he now decided he would move on to electric communication. Turning his back on the fame and wealth that surely awaited if he explored the commercial aspects of his invention, he went back to his beloved research, working on a host of projects including, of course, methods of communication using electricity.

In 1854, he patented a system of wireless telegraphy through water and gave a demonstration of underwater telegraphy by sending a wireless transmission two miles across the River Tay, using the river itself as the connecting medium.

Lindsay also came up with a telegraphic dictionary where, with the use of binary combinations, 24 simple signals could give 331,776 signals, more than all the words in the dictionaries of that time. He went on to describe how a submarine cable could link America with the UK and how electric welding could join the cables. As far as is known, this is the first ever reference to such a process, giving Lindsay yet another string to his electric bow.

At this point, the fledgling field of transatlantic communications, including the difficulties of laying cable, had not been solved, halting the commercial potential of what Lindsay was investigating. But there is no doubt that Lindsay saw the immense possibilities that they presented. He wrote in his lecture notes:

> Intelligence from Australia, instead of taking months, will
> arrive in as many minutes and we may hold personal
> conversations with our friends in New Zealand . . . Sent from
> the copper it [electricity] circumnavigates the world . . . the
> network of wire is destined to be spread above or interred
> beneath the surface of the earth.

He then added:

> The scattered sons of Adam will thus be reunited in a single
> family and they will read with horror the black catalogue of
> their hostilities. Their swords will then be turned into
> ploughshares and their spears into pruning hooks, and the

> other implements of war exhibited in the museum as a
> specimen of bygone barbarism.

Which goes to show that he wasn't right about everything.

Once again, James Bowman Lindsay found himself at the forefront of a scientific revolution. Had he continued, the likes of Marconi and Morse might have been relegated to footnotes in history. But once again, he did not pursue his scientific investigations. Instead, he turned his massive intellect towards his great love of theology and painstakingly began work on the production of a Pentecontaglossal Dictionary of 50 languages, a process through which he intended to shed light on the origins of man and prove the accuracy of the Bible. He also worked on a 'Chrono-Astrolabe' – a gargantuan and ultimately fruitless task of creating a full set of astronomical tables to calculate chronological periods.

Lindsay was a deeply religious and humane man. He turned down a prestigious and well-paying post at the British Museum in order to stay in Dundee and care for his aged mother, the woman who had worked tirelessly to raise the money required to give her son a proper education.

Lindsay finally gained a belated recognition for his efforts when in 1858, at the recommendation of the Prime Minister, Queen Victoria granted him a pension of £100 per year.

He died four years later.

Lindsay's dedication to research rather than wealth or recognition doomed him to obscurity. The electric light, which could have made him a household name, was never one of his passions – his ambition to come up with it stemmed mainly from a desire to provide non-flammable illumination for Dundee's Jute mills, where workers often died as the result of flash fires.

There have been doubts cast by some scientists on the authenticity of Lindsay's 'electric light' – there have been suggestions that what he discovered was merely an unrecognised form of arc lighting. One look at Lindsay's astonishing life and career should be enough to allay those doubts. Despite the futility of projects like the Pentecontaglossal Dictionary and the Chrono-Astrolabe, Bowman's true genius showed itself in pure science and especially in his investigations of electricity.

James Bowman Lindsay was easily experienced enough to know whether or not he had produced real electric light. More tellingly, when one looks at Lindsay's life, and the kind of man he was, it seems obvious that he would not lie about it.

If James Bowman Lindsay said he invented the electric light, he did.

GODS AND MONSTERS

My devil had been long caged, he came out roaring.
ROBERT LOUIS STEVENSON, *DR JEKYLL AND MR HYDE*

The Scots have some admirable literary achievements under their belts. The first editor of the *Oxford English Dictionary* was Scotsman James Murray, the first edition of the *Encyclopaedia Britannica* was compiled, edited and printed in Edinburgh, and the (Scottish) King James version of the Bible is the most used book in the English language.

Scots founded *Forbes Magazine, The New York Tribune, New York Herald, The Toronto Globe, The Boston Chronicle, The Spectator* and *The Economist.* They produced the first English bible in the US, the first newspaper printed in North America and came up with the modern book jacket.

Scots also produced some very respectable writers. Around 1500, Gavin Douglas (1476–1522), Bishop of Dunkeld, was the first person to translate the *Aeneid*, along with other Latin classics, into English. James Boswell (1740–95) wrote the superb biography, *Life of Johnson*, in 1791. One of Britain's great historians and philosophers, Thomas Carlyle

(1795–1881), wrote *The French Revolution* and *The Life of Fredrick the Great*. John Stuart Mill (1806–73), author of *On Liberty*, was the son of the Scottish intellectual James Mill and had a huge impact on Victorian thought. A study in the '70s estimated his IQ at around 200, which would make it the highest in history.

While this is an admirable litany of literary achievements, it's not exactly one that changed the world. Scots writers like James Hogg, Robert Fergusson, Edwin Muir, Hugh MacDiarmid, Norman MacCaig, Edwin Morgan, John Buchan, George Mackay Brown, John McGrath, John Byrne, Iain Banks, Liz Lochhead and Ian Rankin are well respected and cover many genres, but they're not exactly quoted in the pub.

However, there is an area in which the influence of Scotland is well and truly underestimated.

Fantasy writing.

Fantasy writing conjures up unfortunate stereotypical images of dragons, knights, and computer geeks. But literary fantasy involving Scotland covers a massive range of topics, time spans and scenarios – and perhaps this is the reason its immense impact has been overlooked. Some of the most famous fantasies covered here were not even written by Scots, but they were greatly influenced by Scotland.

The Scots fantasy explosion dates from the eighteenth century – even Robert Burns had a go. Though he is not considered a fantasy writer, his most famous poem, *Tam O' Shanter*, concerns a drunken race against a bunch of witches – not exactly an everyday occurrence.

Walter Scott, of course, is the grandfather of Scottish fantasy writing. Novels like *Rob Roy*, *The Heart of Midlothian* and *Redgauntlet* portray a heather-covered paradise stocked with noble Highland warriors – to say he was viewing Scotland's past through rose-coloured glasses is an understatement. Scott's popularity waxed and waned over the years but, while he lived, he was the most famous man in Europe. His fantastic portrayal of Scotland was, literally, as famous as he was.

But why was the connection between fantasy writing and Scotland so prevalent from the eighteenth century onward, and why did it gain such an international popularity?

The answer lies in Scotland's history. It was a country dealt a massive social rabbit punch. As Highland Scots were driven overseas by extreme hardship, war or land clearance, their ancestral home assumed mythic proportions. The sense of losing a place that had been theirs since the dawn of time leant the Highlands a surreal quality. 'You don't know what you've got till it's gone' is a true phrase indeed.

Back in Scotland, the lowlander suffered the equally dispiriting indignity of the Industrial Revolution and longed for the simpler rural life of the past. Though he may never have seen it, the wild untamed areas of Scotland now represented all that he never had.

The fact that life had always been hard in Scotland was forgotten. In the minds of Scots, the 'old country' became a glorious never-never land. Because they lived it, they knew how to tell it – and the rest of the world listened in awe. Knowing that somewhere across the ocean lay Fantasy Island with heather was somehow comforting.

Scotland was a 'thin place' – a land where fantasy and reality might actually be able to mix. People need that kind of hope.

The level of fantasy varied from writer to writer. Compton McKenzie, S.R. Crockett, John Watson and J.M. Barrie portrayed quaint, idealised visions of Scotland in books like *Whisky Galore*, *A Window in Thrums* and the *Little Minister*. These books were derisively labelled as Kailyard stories and were usually set in some pre-industrial utopian village, peopled with solid, hard-working decent types for whom everything always turned out all right in the end.

Derided or not, they were immensely popular in England and America and helped shape those countries' idea of Scotland as a quaint collection of heathery hamlets, rather than the tough, industrial and economically challenged society it was.

The Scots fantasy was keenly aware of the realities of growing up in such a harsh country, and compensated with stunning children's fantasies. Kenneth Graham wrote the children's classic *Wind in the Willows* while living in Edinburgh and Robert Louis Stevenson penned a series of immortal children's fantasy poems under the title *A Child's Garden of Verses*. And, of course, J.M. Barrie wrote *Peter Pan*, creating some of the seminal images of the twentieth century.

The boy who never grew up lives, like all the other 'lost boys', in never-never land – the Scotland of the imagination.

In the twenty-first century, Scotland is back at the forefront of children's fantasy, with the astonishing success of J.K. Rowling's *Harry Potter* books.

In movies dealing with Scotland, elements of fantasy and kailyard were equally strong – and just as well-liked. There are some excellent hard-hitting movies about Scotland, but they never stood a chance in the popularity stakes. Instead, quaint semi-fantasies like *Whisky Galore*, *Geordie*, and *The Maggie* dominated the public view of Scotland, while *Brigadoon* is jaw-droppingly over-the-top in creating a mythical Scottish village. Even 'historical' films like *Bonnie Prince Charlie* bore no resemblance to the harsh reality of the Jacobite campaigns and movies with a definite social message like Alexander McKendrick's *The Man in the White Suit* presented this 'realism' in a science fiction format.

In more modern times, the trend is the same, Bill Forsyth gave Scotland an intelligent mix of social realism, kailyard cuteness and surreal imagery in films like *Gregory's Girl*, *Local Hero* and *Comfort and Joy*. *Highlander* presented the world with Frenchman Christopher Lambert playing an immortal clansman, striding across the heather to the strains of 'Who Wants to Live Forever' – an image that reduces viewers to tears for many different reasons. The real Scotsman in the film, Sean Connery ends up playing a Spaniard. There are those who claim, rather ungenerously, that portraying Scotland as a fantasyland has continued in movies like *Braveheart* and *Rob Roy*.

The recent exception would seem to be the bleak, violent and controversial film *Trainspotting* – until one remembers the baby crawling across the roof and the journey down through the world's worst toilet – and the fact that it's a black comedy about heroin addiction.

In real life, Scotland has always been a brutal and bloody nation. Its dark side may be polished till it dazzles, but it can't be denied. And Scotland's second popular literary vein runs right into that jugular of darkness. Peer into the hidden corners of Scotland's past and some of world's most terrifying and influential monsters come crawling out.

In 1816 Mary Shelley, Percy Shelley, Lord Byron, and Dr John Polidori, held a party at the Villa Diodoti on the shores of Lake Geneva, where they decided to write a horror story each. It's ironic but somehow satisfactory that neither of the arch-egotists, Byron or Percy Shelley, came up with anything decent. Polidori, on the other hand, wrote a short story named *The Vampyre* and Mary Shelly, aged 19, wrote the immortal *Frankenstein*.

It is popularly thought that Mary Shelley's inspiration for the story of Frankenstein comes from her husband's callous treatment of her miscarriage. What is less well known is that Mary Shelley (then Woolstonecraft) grew up in Dundee – and then, after marrying Percy Shelley, honeymooned in Edinburgh. This places Mary Shelley firmly in Scotland, when it led the world in scientific and medical advances, and when the unfortunate profession of body snatching was at its most virulent. Men would sneak into the graveyards at night and dig up corpses to sell to the anatomists of Edinburgh, who would then experiment on them.

Sounds familiar, doesn't it?

Though it is originally a creature from Slavic folklore, Polidori wrote what is considered to be the first true vampire story, appropriately titled *The Vampyre*. But he based his protagonist on Byron, who went to school in Aberdeen. The vampire legend then achieved everlasting fame with the publication of the novel *Dracula*. Bram Stoker wrote the novel in Scotland.

Scotland is a land of duality. Natives of the rugged Highlands and the rolling Lowlands have a history of mutual antipathy. Glasgow was an industrial giant, while Edinburgh was the city of enlightenment. In religion, temperament and actions Scots have demonstrated this duality of character more strongly than any other nation – and a veneer of respectability and romanticism has been thickly layered over an aggressive and often barbaric people.

Scottish writer Arthur Conan Doyle managed to portray this in his creation of *Sherlock Holmes* – based on the respected Scots surgeon, Joseph Bell, a lecturer at Edinburgh Medical College. Holmes is a master of logical thinking, yet melancholy and drug addicted – and he comes up against a number of memorable villains who are rather similar to him.

Of all Scottish writers, however, Robert Louis Stevenson (1850–94) captured the duality of Scotland most brilliantly. He was not above romanticising his own land, *The Master of Ballantrae* and *Kidnapped* are proof of that. But Stevenson could see the dichotomy in his own mythologizing, writing:

> The happiest lot on earth is to be born a Scotsman. You must pay for it in many ways, as for all other advantages on earth . . . you generally take to drink, your youth, as far as I can find out, is a time of louder war against society, of more outcry and tears and turmoil, than if you had been born, for instance, in England. But somehow life is warmer and closer; the hearth burns more redly, the lights of home shine softer on the rainy street, the very names, endeared in verse and music, cling nearer round our hearts.

Stevenson was a sickly man who was well aware of his own mortality, and his romantic fantasy was tempered by the unpleasant and realistic aspects of the swashbuckling life – that wonderful tale, *Treasure Island* is downright scary in parts.

But in one novel, Stevenson displayed perfectly the duality of the Scottish nation and its people, and by putting that duality into one man he finally voiced a universally recognised fear. Inspired by the life of a real Scottish character, Deacon William Brodie, Stevenson penned the immortal *Dr Jekyll and Mr Hyde* in 1886.

Dr Jekyll and Mr Hyde is not just a famous story. It had a profound effect on the way the human race saw itself. Henry Jekyll is torn between his 'good' self and the desire we all have to do whatever we want. He concocts a powder that will separate the two sides in the hope of freeing his life of 'all that was unbearable'. Unfortunately, he also frees his alter ego, Mr Hyde, in the process. Jekyll makes the huge mistake of assuming that it is possible for one side of his nature to do without the other and, in the end, is forced to end his own life along with Hyde's.

On the surface this is just a chilling gothic horror story, but underneath is actually an astonishingly perceptive study of the nature of human evil, a study that has obsessed man since the dawn of history. Even those who have never read the book grasp its concept instantly as an idea of universal significance. Written in three days, it anticipates the famed works of Freud and Jung by decades.

Stevenson almost seems to have understood the biological significance of humankind's dilemma. Hyde is not evil, he is simply callous. He is not bad, just totally without empathy. It is an almost perfect description of the relationship between the gene and the body. As the anthropologist Lyall Watson pointed out, Stevenson 'perfectly catches the feeling of genetic self-absorption and short sighted concern'.

If one doubts the influence of this monumental book, one only has to look at Freud's 'Id', or the writings of Carl Jung, who stated 'I must have a dark side also if I am to be whole; and inasmuch as I become conscious of my shadow I also remember that I am a human being like any other.'

Frankenstein has almost the same duality. Dr Frankenstein rejects his creation when he realises it is not the perfect being he was aiming for, and denies all responsibility for his actions. In disowning the dark side of his deeds he brings disaster upon himself.

Both books have become iconic and shaped the world's conception about the good and bad in us all – as well as providing the ultimate in cautionary tales about playing God. In these times of genetic engineering and modification, the whole of western civilisation's attitudes towards today's monumental scientific possibilities are shaped by the stories *Dr Jekyll and Mr Hyde* and *Frankenstein*.

The duality of life in Scotland, experienced first hand by Stevenson and Shelley, have now become humankind's yardstick when considering the dangers of scientific experimentation and the fundamental nature of identity.

Quite ironic, then, that the greatest genetic step ever taken – the world's first clone – was produced in Edinburgh.

Through a slew of popular fantasy literature, the Scot has managed to become savage, noble, taciturn, hard working, pragmatic, generous, mean and wily. He is a hero and an antihero. And he lives in a wonderful land, where the rest of the world would like to live, which may or may not exist. The nearest parallel, once again, is the North American Indian, that other great mythological tribe. If the Scots influence is greater, it's only because they were allowed to adapt and mythologize themselves rather than being hunted to near extinction.

The Scotland admired so much today is the one portrayed in book and film. Fortunately, there is enough beauty and friendliness in that country to capture a part of that fantasy – no mean feat. Fantasies are notoriously hard to live up to.

Yet the destruction of old buildings to make way for underground malls, the rising racism disguised as nationalism, the reliance on history to impress rather than being impressive in the present – all these take their toll on that ideal vision.

Scotland must be careful: it cannot claim to be the wonderful place it has been portrayed unless its people intend to live up to that fantasy.

In Canada, for instance, children really do play bagpipes in the back garden and the shops are not adorned by dolls wearing tartan skirts. There, the inhabitants are fiercely proud to be Scots without having to drunkenly sing a national anthem they only know the first verse of to prove it. They try to live up to the myth that was created in their ancestral homeland.

We should, at least, attempt to do the same.

BROADCAST NEWS

Winning isn't everything, but wanting to win is.
VINCENT LOMBARDI (1913-70), US FOOTBALL COACH

In 1895, Guglielmo Marconi (1874–1937), achieved lasting world fame when he made the first-ever radio communication. A year later, in England, he conducted experiments that led to the formation of the Marconi Wireless Telegraph Company Ltd. Marconi went on to convert radio waves into electric signals and began to broadcast those waves over longer and longer distances. In 1908, he transmitted signals across the English Channel. By 1918 his radio reached from England to Australia.

His achievements won him the Nobel Prize for Physics in 1909.

Guglielmo Marconi was no stranger to controversy. For a start, the apparatus he used was simply an improvement on equipment designed by the German physicist Heinrich Hertz. In turn, Hertz's own experiments were merely confirming the Scotsman James Clerk Maxwell's theory of electromagnetic waves.

In 1912, Marconi's company became embroiled in a major political scandal – UK chancellor Lloyd George and two government ministers were found to have dealt in shares of the US Marconi Company shortly before the British Post Office accepted a bid by the UK Marconi Company to construct an imperial wireless chain.

A parliamentary select committee was set up to determine whether the appointment of UK Marconi was the result of political shenanigans. The committee, heavily biased towards the Liberal Government, declared that the other four wireless systems in the running had been discounted because they were technically inadequate. Though the investigation ended there, it was widely rumoured that the whole thing was a fix, and Lloyd George's reputation was irreparably damaged.

A few years later Marconi was back in the wars, involved in a ferocious two-year tussle with Baird Television for the contract to operate television for the British Broadcasting Company. Marconi won – and the Scotsman, Baird, the first person to demonstrate a televised picture, lost his final foothold in the industry he had pioneered.

Given the might of the Marconi Company and the speed at which it grew into a corporate giant, it's understandable that the achievements of other wireless pioneers might have been somewhat overshadowed.

Like the fact that a Scots inventor broadcast a radio message a year before Marconi did.

Andrew Muirhead, from East Lothian, was an electrical engineer working on cable telegraph systems, when he joined forces with Sir Oliver Lodge, professor of Physics at University College, Liverpool. The two men were intrigued by the idea of sending radio messages and began experiments to transmit wireless messages, working on the same principles as Marconi himself.

On 14 August 1894, Muirhead and Lodge successfully transmitted a wireless Morse Code message from the Clarendon Physics building at Oxford University to a receiver at the Museum of Natural History, 100 metres away.

Though their achievement was momentous, Muirhead and Lodge did not publicise what they had done; in fact, they didn't even bother to write down the Morse code message they sent. Although aware of the vast potential of their achievement, they intended to fine tune their invention before unleashing it on an admiring world.

They were too late. Only a year later, Marconi demonstrated and patented the same technology in a blaze of publicity, taking all the credit for its invention. Muirhead and Lodge, the first transmitters of a wireless message, vanished into obscurity.

It was probably no consolation to them that Marconi, though born in Bologna, was of Scottish ancestry.

THE FLYING SCOTSMEN

The airplane stays up because it doesn't have the time to fall.
ORVILLE WRIGHT (1871–1948), DEMONSTRATING HIS GRASP OF PHYSICS

On 17 December 1903, the Wright brothers flew their powered glider, *Kittyhawk*, over the sands at Kitty Hawk Bay in the United States. As everyone knows, this was the first ever manned flight of a heavier-than-air machine.

Or was it?

The Scots were remarkable inventors in their day but their influence had waned by the early twentieth century. They are certainly not associated with one of the greatest innovations of that era – aviation. Yet, in the race for the skies, the Scots may well have crossed the finishing line first, thanks to the efforts of two individuals: one famous, one completely unknown.

Alexander Graham Bell is an unlikely candidate for fame as an aviator. Born in Charlotte Square, Edinburgh, he will always be famous as the inventor of the telephone – but Bell had many irons in his creative fire. He invented the tetrahedron and the hydrofoil and developed his own methods of teaching the deaf to speak. There was no sphere of science that didn't interest him.

Having made his fortune, Bell settled in Nova Scotia and began a number of wide-ranging experiments, including investigations into kites, propellers and flying machines. While working on the telephone, Bell had already mentioned to Watson that their next project would be a flying machine and by 1891, he was testing helicopter models and kites.

Bell joined forces with his friend Simon Pierpont Langley and together they made a series of powered model planes which were capable of flying up to a quarter of a mile. The models worked perfectly, proving that heavier air machines were certainly capable of flight. All Bell and Langley had to do was get one off the ground – with a man sitting in it.

Bell, however, was reluctant to be associated with manned, powered flight. In the eyes of the scientific community, this ranked with time-travel and turning lead into gold as a reputation sinker and Bell didn't want his impeccable status tarnished. Langley had no such qualms.

In 1903, nine days before the Wright brothers flew the *Kittyhawk*, the Bell–Langley flying machine made its bid to master the skies.

It crashed.

Bell had wisely kept his name away from the project but Langley had welcomed publicity and now suffered the brunt of public ridicule. Bell reacted by stating his belief, afterwards, that this massive communal derision was responsible for Langley's early death. Ironically, Wilbur and Orville Wright made their flight in secret to prevent the same public ridicule if they failed. Their success, of course, vindicated Langley and he was recognised posthumously as one of aviation's pioneers.

Once flight had been proved possible, however, Bell was able to openly experiment with aeroplanes. In 1907, he helped form the Ariel Experiment Association and developed a series of machines which would make aviation history. On 23 February 1909, his plane, the *Silver Dart*, flew half a mile over frozen Bras d'Or Lake near Baddeck – the first manned flight in Canada. Though a great achievement, the *Silver Dart* flew four years after the *Kittyhawk* – and the first-ever Canadian flight didn't exactly shake the world.

Posterity has come down on the side of the Wright Brothers, mainly because the Bell–Langley plane crashed and the *Kittyhawk* didn't. Yet the Smithsonian Institution in Washington called the Bell–Langley machine 'The first flying machine in the history of the world capable of flight with a man', and displayed Bell's plane, rather than the Wrights' *Kittyhawk*, for almost 50 years.

Even if Bell is denied credit for the first manned flight, Scotland has an unknown contender for the prize – a man called Preston Watson.

Preston Watson was born in 1880, the son of a Dundee merchant. He grew up to be a fine athlete, but his passion was the dynamics of flying. Observing gliding birds, he noticed that they turned in the air by dipping one wing and allowing the opposite wing to lift. Inspired by this, he began to build his own 'flying machines', using the same principle to control their flights.

Watson designed a rigid monoplane fitted with a smaller upper plane. He could tilt this upper 'parasol plane' to either side, causing the whole machine to bank right or left. This method of control was simpler and more structurally sound than the Wright brothers' design, which depended on the plane's wings being twisted or warped. Unfortunately, only French aviators recognised this achievement at the time by giving Watson an award.

Preston Watson began his flying experiments by building a full-scale glider using this revolutionary principle. In 1903 he attempted a flight at Errol, near the banks of the river Tay – the site, appropriately enough, is now an RAF aerodrome.

Since Watson's glider was taking off from ground level, he had to come up with some way of actually getting his contraption *off* the ground. To do so, he invented a device unique in the annals of aviation. He put the glider on skids, which could slide freely along planks lubric-ated with lard. A rope, hooked under the glider, led forward to a pulley, back under the plane, round another pulley and, finally, up and over the branch of a tall tree. On the end of this rope hung two 56lb weights and an anvil borrowed from a nearby smithy. Using a catch under his seat, Watson caused the weights to fall, catapulting his machine into the air. This may sound more like a suicide attempt than a flight attempt, but he made it. Eye-witnesses later described the resounding crash of falling weights as Watson shot into the sky.

Having survived the lethal combination of home-made catapult and glider, Watson's next task was to find a light engine which was powerful enough to turn his glider into a plane. The Wright brothers had found it necessary to design and build their own motor, but Preston Watson's chosen method of propulsion is unclear. Records show that in 1906, two years after the Wright brothers, he bought an air-cooled petrol engine from the French aviation pioneer, Santos Dumont. However, this does not seem to be Watson's first method of propulsion.

Dundee craftsman, Kerr Sturrock, made over a dozen wooden propellers for Watson *before* 1905. Sturrock claimed these propellers were fitted to small De Dion motors, two of which were coupled together on Watson's plane. These first propellers were made of oak or yellow pine and broke easily, until Sturrock began shaping them from laminated layers of Australian walnut. This new method of propeller manufacture was so successful that it remained the aviation industry's choice until alloy replaced wood in World War I.

Sturrock never gave a precise date for Watson's first flight using the De Dion motors and his own walnut propellers. Yet a 1957 investigation found and interviewed agricultural workers who had watched Watson's plane making short flights over the fields of Errol where they were labouring. It was not a mere glider Preston Watson was flying this time – the workers could hear the drone of the craft's engine.

They gave the dates of these flights as 1903–4.

If they were correct, Preston Watson flew *before* the Wright brothers. Encouraged by the success of his early experiments, Watson continued to build better and better planes and his craft were often seen flying over Tayside in the years immediately before World War I. When hostilities did break out, Watson volunteered for service with the newly formed Royal Naval Air Service.

Barely two months after obtaining his commission, the plane he was flying exploded in mid-air.

He was 35 years old.

There will always be debate over whether Bell's machine can be called a proper flight, or if it was merely a crash in progress. In the same way, we'll never know if Watson really did beat the Wright brothers or if he just came a close second.

But when a new science as exciting as aviation came along – one that required engineering skills, craftsmanship and practical thinking to progress properly – there shouldn't have been any doubt that Scots would be at the forefront of the development.

THE MEAN MACHINE

If folk think I'm mean, they'll no expect too much.
SIR HARRY LAUDER (1870–1950)

Highlanders, it is reputed, are prone to melancholy. If you've ever been up to the Highlands in winter, it isn't difficult to see why. Lowlanders, on the other hand, are simply dour.

True or not, the Scots, as a nation, have a far more famous character flaw. Scots are stingy. Tight-fisted. Miserable about money. The sombre tone of Scottish Presbyterianism, and the urge of pious hard-working Scotsmen to 'get on' has often led to a charge of national meanness.

But is there any truth in the stereotype?

The Highland Scot can certainly be cleared of this accusation. Most of the highlanders were Catholic until the Reformation, and surely the most guilt-free bunch of Catholics ever to walk God's earth. They were often short of money, but money wasn't of prime importance. If they really needed something they could always take it from someone else. Despite the extreme poverty of the north,

Highland hospitality is legendary. This is not a reputation that could have blossomed in an ungenerous culture.

It must be the lowlander, then, who condemned Scotland to an endless stream of jokes about being able to catch a dropped penny from the other side of the room. Yet a closer look at Presbyterian philosophy does not reveal a reluctance to part with hard-earned cash – it is more an abhorrence of 'wasting' money. The Presbyterians didn't have any objection to spending, just to spending immorally or idly. It was quite acceptable to splash out on books, education or deserving causes and it was also customary to provide hospitality without begrudging it. That this hospitality didn't extend to a case of beer and a trip to the brothel is a reflection of the Lowland Scot's moral values, not an indication of meanness to part with cash.

In fact, the Scot reputation for meanness is pretty much the product of one man – Sir Harry Lauder.

There are many who despise the name of Harry Lauder, for more reasons than one. As a stage entertainer, his portrayal of the kilted, homespun highlander horrified many Scots: the poet Hugh MacDiarmid, for instance, regarded Lauder with 'despair and disgust'. Yet Harry Lauder did more than just ham up some of the more questionable Scottish characteristics.

He had the power to make the world think they were real.

Far less famous now than in his heyday, Lauder is remembered mainly from scratchy old records and faded photographs. The pictures show a little man with bow legs who bears more than a passing resemblance to Stan Laurel. Sporting a kilt, a flat bonnet with an enormous feather and a knobbly stick, he poses in front of an equally fake Highland music hall backdrop.

As well as being a vaudeville star, Lauder was a popular writer, producing slices of homespun acumen with excruciating titles like *Folks that Get my Goat, Gi'e Me the Lass that's Plump* and *Books I'd Like Fine to Read Again*. He dispensed pearls of wisdom like 'The highbrow is not a man with a big forehead. He is usually an individual obsessed with a big idea. That big idea is – himself.'

Lauder never claimed to be a profound wit. His observations came straight from the heart and he couldn't be faulted for that. But homely Highland philosophy *à la* Lauder can still send a shiver down the spine of the most hardened liberal.

His advice to women, for instance, is a feminist nightmare:

> Take plenty of exercise, eat cannily, be sparin wi' the
> chocolates, and they'll be nae fears o' ye becoming unwieldy.
> You'll just be that Buxom, sonsy, cheerful body we men a' like
> to see. As I've said already, I like a womanly woman. Nane o'
> your walking-stick for Harry Lauder.

On the other hand, another version of the same sentiment seems
remarkably appropriate today:

> I don't like this slimming business. It's no natural . . . It's an
> absurd, nay, a tragic, business when fashion fads interfere
> with the shape o' the human body.

A lesson which fashion designers and supermodels should take to heart.

Henry McLennan Lauder was born in 1870, in the village of Porto-
bello, just outside Edinburgh. His family wasn't poor, but he ended
up working in a flax mill, then a coal mine, where his singing
prompted co-workers to enter him in a competition. He came second,
but decided that a life on the boards was far preferable to life under
them.

Lauder went from strength to strength. After becoming famous in
Scotland he toured the world for 40 years, including 22 trips to the
USA and several to Australia. Eventually his name was known across
the globe and Sir Winston Churchill referred to him as 'Scotland's
greatest-ever ambassador'.

Lauder achieved fame at just the right time in history. As the
nineteenth century moved into the twentieth it was possible, for the
first time, that a performer could become a megastar – Lauder was the
first British artist to sell a million records. He wrote most of his own
songs and anthems like 'Roamin' in the Gloamin'', 'I Love a Lassie', 'A
Wee Deoch-an-Doris', and 'Keep Right on to the End of the Road' –
love them or hate them – are still famous today.

Lauder also appeared in the motion pictures *Huntingtower* (1928),
Auld Lang Syne (1929) and *The End of the Road* (1936) and his books
such as *Harry Lauder at Home and on Tour* (1912), *A Minstrel in France*
(1918), *Roamin' in the Gloamin'* (1927), *My Best Scotch Stories* (1929), *Wee
Drappies* (1931) and *Ticklin' Talks* (1932) were immensely popular.

Harry Lauder was still going strong when World War I broke out.
Too old to fight, he raised huge sums of money for war charities and
entertained troops in the trenches – even coming under enemy fire.

Lauder's only child, John, was not so lucky. He was killed at Poiziers, France in 1916.

After one day of mourning Lauder went back to his show – solely to keep the cast in much needed employment. He gave a flawless performance then collapsed when the curtain fell.

After the war ended, he was given a knighthood.

During World War II Lauder was back again, entertaining troops on the radio. He even turned up at Glasgow docks to publicly thank the crews of American relief ships, though he was almost 80 years old.

Sir Harry Lauder died 26 February 1950. Pathé News covered his funeral and wreaths were received from all over the world, including one from the Queen Mother and another from Mr & Mrs Winston Churchill.

All his life Harry Lauder was known for his generosity. During World War I he hired 100 pipers, at his own expense, to march the length and breadth of Scotland recruiting soldiers. Throughout his long career, he never demanded fees but took whatever was offered. Despite this, he still managed to become the highest paid entertainer of his time.

Lauder always played the same character – the homely highlander with a ridiculous tartan outfit and rolling accent straight out of the hills. It was all an act, of course – Lauder was a lowlander from a comfortably-off family.

But the most famous part of his fake Scottish persona was his insistence that he was mean. In real life Lauder was the epitome of generosity but this tight-fistedness was the mainstay of an act that lasted almost 60 years.

The Scots comedian Stanley Baxter (1926–) summed up exactly why the ultra-popular Lauder is now frowned upon by so many of his countrymen:

> The legend that Scots are mean originated with Sir Harry Lauder when he was a low comedian before becoming that 'grand old minstrel' as Churchill had it. Because of the awful image of the Scot Lauder gave the world, his memory is not exactly revered by many. The smear of meanness has become a crashing bore to millions of Scots who never saw Lauder.

Sir Harry Lauder was loved by millions and was one of the first global superstars: the advent of modern technology and international travel made him a household name. He was the first Scotsman that the world could experience first hand. And he convinced the world that Scotsmen were mean.

It believed him. It still does.

HARD TO SWALLOW

Freedom an' whisky gang thegither.

ROBERT BURNS

Whisky is famous as the Scots national drink and it is widely accepted that whisky has been distilled in the country for hundreds of years. The origins of the famed *uisge beatha*, or 'water of life', are unclear: it may have been brought into the country by missionaries from Ireland. Since Muslims were among the first to learn distillation techniques, knights from the Crusades – perhaps even the Knights Templar – could also have brought the knowledge back from the Crusades with them. The beginnings of the famous drink may be simpler than this, however. Whisky may have been a means of using up barley that would otherwise have been ruined after a wet harvest.

The Gaelic name is derived from the Latin *aqua vitae*, a spirit common in Europe. It made its first appearance in official Scottish records in 1494, with a record of malt being sold to one Friar John Cor. Oddly enough, the religious orders remained the main distillers until the dissolution of many monasteries in the sixteenth century, when Highland clans began to produce it in primitive stills. It was, predictably enough, a rough and unrefined drink and bore no resemblance to the refined beverage that connoisseurs now enjoy all over the world.

Whisky was not produced in any great quantity in Scotland until the eighteenth and early nineteenth centuries, and then the severe taxes imposed on the licensed manufacture of the drink encouraged illicit stills and smuggling. It was not until the 1823 Excise Act actually lowered the tax on spirits, that homemade 'moonshine' went into decline. It was cheaper and less risky to buy a distillery licence for £10 than to continue 'free trading'.

Most of the whisky empires that we know today date from this period. In the nineteenth century, Robert Stein and Aeneas Coffey invented a patent still which enabled the continuous distillation of whisky and allowed the drink to be mass produced. It also marked the beginning of the famous Scottish distilleries like Johnnie Walker, Dewar's and Bell's.

In the 1870s, the phylloxera infestation of French vineyards decimated brandy production in France and blended Scotch whisky was marketed to fill the gap in England's drinking. The resulting whisky boom heralded a huge expansion in the industry, and blended whisky was exported to all corners of the British Empire.

Lowland Scots, however, continued to drink mainly wine and claret – whisky only became acceptable when the Napoleonic wars made it too difficult to get hold of French tipple. Portuguese wine was too bitter, so Scots traders added brandy to it, resulting in the quintessential English drink, port – and they drank that too, in preference to whisky.

Even in the Highlands whisky was drunk sparingly. The northern clansmen's normal beverage was ale – the water of life was held in high reverence and used for special occasions.

Only the Lowland working-class Scot drank whisky in any great amount, but during the eighteenth and nineteenth centuries, the working class would drink any spirit they could get their hands on. This was not appreciation of the liqueur itself, but rather to get drunk as quickly as possible to forget the desperation of industrial life.

Even today, whisky is not the preferred drink of the working man. Sales of lager in Scotland vastly exceed sales of any other alcoholic drink.

There is no denying that whisky occupies a very special place in Scottish history and culture, but this is largely due to its links with the legendary romanticism of the Highlands. As the diplomat Bruce Lockhart (1887–1970) put it:

> Whisky has made us what we are. It goes with our climate and
> our nature. It rekindles old fires in us, our hatred of cant and
> privilege, and above all, our love of Scotland.

But it only became nationally popular as a drink when the Victorians
put it on a pedestal along with tartan, kilts and bagpipes.

To the world, Scots and whisky now go together like Abbott and
Costello – even though Abbott and Costello didn't particularly like each
other. Scots hold whisky in the utmost esteem – it is an icon, and a superb
one at that – but a large proportion of the public never touch it.

The Scots are not a nation of whisky drinkers, but a nation of
whisky producers. To say it's our national drink is a bit like saying tea
is the national drink of Ceylon. It isn't. It's just where lots of it is made.

Scots even aided whisky manufacture in other countries. James Crow
(1800–59), a graduate physician from Edinburgh, vastly improved the
American methods of distilling whisky with his sour mash process and is
generally given credit for founding the modern Bourbon whiskey industry.

But Scotland, oddly enough, provided the inspiration for what might be
termed the world's national drink – if, of course, you discount water –
Coca-Cola.

An article in the *Mineral Water Trade Review* of 1873 makes the first
written reference to a 'Kola'-type drink. In it there is a
recommendation for drinks manufacturers to use the seeds of the Kola
nut to form a syrup for lemonade. Kola was a popular drink in Scotland
as early as the nineteenth century and several Scottish drinks companies manufacturing Kola at the time do so to this day. In fact, Scotland
is the only country today that still has the drink called 'Kola' – traditionally known in the drinks trade as 'Scotch Kola'. In 1879, however,
an American trade writer recorded this report:

> In Scotland they have a drink called Kola in which extracts from
> the nuts and leaves of the African Cola tree are used. It is much
> thought of by the natives and flavoured in various ways by the

fashion of meads, sherberts [sic] and sherries. It could presumably be tried in the United States by any enterprising bottler.

Around this time, American drinks manufacturers had been experimenting with coca-flavoured drinks derived from the leaves of the Brazilian coca shrub. Proof of this comes from two American chemists who entered into a rather bad-tempered correspondence with each other in the late 1870s, both claiming to be the originator of the coca drink.

In 1884 or 1885 the American chemist, John Pemberton, came up with the idea of combining the flavours of Coca and Scotch Kola to produce a new blend of soft drink.

The drink went into manufacture as Coca-Cola.

ONE HUMP OR TWO?

The bigger they come, the harder they fall.
BOB FITZSIMMONS (1862–1917), HEAVYWEIGHT BOXER

In 1932 a newspaper report appeared in the *Inverness Courier* recording an intriguing incident on the shore of Loch Ness. According to the local reporter, Alex Campbell, a 'well-known Inverness businessman and his wife' saw an unidentified creature thrashing about in the loch.

> The lady was the first to notice the disturbance, which occurred fully three quarters of a mile from the shore, and it was her sudden cries to stop that drew her husband's attention to the water.
>
> There, the creature disported itself, rolling and plunging for fully a minute, its body resembling that of a whale, and the water cascading and churning like a simmering cauldron. Soon, however it disappeared in a boiling mass of foam.

The rest is, as they say, is history.

Except . . . that wasn't exactly how it happened. The couple were actually Mr and Mrs Mackay from Drumnadrochit, a village close to the loch. Mrs Mackay admitted later that the disturbance was only a hundred yards away and seemed to be caused by 'two ducks fighting'. Mr Mackay didn't see anything at all – he was too busy concentrating on his driving.

The *Courier* subsequently published an interview with Captain John Macdonald, supervisor of the Loch Ness steamers. He too had seen such disturbances in Loch Ness – which he admitted looked like the thrashing of some monster – until he got closer and saw they were caused by groups of salmon leaping through the water.

Despite follow-up articles by Alex Campbell, who first used the grandiose term 'The Loch Ness Monster', there were only two dubious sightings in the next year.

It looked as though the monster was going to sink without trace.

Then, in August 1933, the *Inverness Courier* published a letter by a Mr Spicer, who claimed to have seen an unidentified creature running across the road bordering the loch. The very next day, the 'monster' was spotted by a local girl called Nellie Smith. A short time later her friend Prudence saw it too. Then it was sighted by one Commander Meikhem and his wife – who just happened to be Alex Campbell's neighbours. Though the Commander didn't reach the loch until an hour after Nellie Smith's sighting, the monster was still there – a rather sociable move for a creature which never again showed itself for more than a few seconds.

Alex Campbell, of course, reported the whole thing in the *Courier* and the monster was back in the public eye.

This prompted even more sightings, but the creature was beginning to show a bewildering array of characteristics.

Spicer had described a 'dragon or prehistoric animal' with a body about 6–8 feet long, carrying a lamb or some other animal in its mouth. He added, rather uncharitably, that it was 'very ugly'. Spicer claimed the creature had a 'long neck' and a 'high back', but could only guess that its lower body might have webbed feet – shrink the whole thing a few feet and it's a pretty good description of an otter carrying its young.

Nellie Smith, on the other hand, stated that the monster had 'huge legs' – while Commander Meikhem then likened it to a large 'horse' with a 'knobbly back'.

Mrs Chesire of Stafford, who furnished the *Courier* with its next sighting, described a large black object she took at first to be 'a piece of shining rock'. Nobody at the *Courier* bothered to point out that she probably *was* looking at a piece of shining rock – the monster sightings, mostly written by Alex Campbell, were becoming too popular as a regular feature in the paper.

In fact, every time public interest waned, a new sighting would pique its curiosity again. The timing was almost uncanny – and it certainly wasn't doing the local tourist trade any harm.

As yet, the monster wasn't national news, but this was to change when city journalist Philip Stalker arrived to investigate for *The Scotsman*. After talking to two witnesses in particular, he became convinced of the monster's existence.

One witness was Alex Campbell. The other was his neighbour, Commander Meikhem.

By this time, Campbell was claiming that he too had seen the monster – which had grown from its original 8 feet to an impressive 30 feet long. Perhaps realising he had gone too far (he also held a responsible job as a water bailiff), Campbell later admitted he had actually seen a flock of birds. He didn't bother to tell Stalker this, however, and in October 1933, *The Scotsman* published what amounted to a summary of Alex Campbell's statements and newspaper articles. Other papers picked up the story and suddenly the Loch Ness Monster was a national celebrity.

Now that the monster's existence was 'established', believers had to work out what 'Nessie' actually was. The most enduring theory was put forward by Lieut.-Commander R.T. Gould that very year. The Loch Ness Monster, he stated confidently, was a plesiosaur – a large aquatic dinosaur that had been extinct for 200 million years everywhere on earth except, apparently, a 23-mile strip of water in Scotland.

Quite naturally, the theory was ignored – until a sensational photograph of the monster by a man named Hugh Gray made the national papers. Countless schoolchildren since have looked at this rather blurred picture and innocently pointed out that it shows a dog's head with a stick – but it didn't matter at the time. The country was gripped with Nessie fever.

No less an institution than *The Times* published Gould's plesiosaur theory. The monster, by this time, had reached 50 feet.

Other papers were not to be outdone. Big-game hunters, hired by the *Daily Mail*, found Nessie's footprints, prompting the headline:

'MONSTER OF LOCH NESS IS NOT A LEGEND BUT A FACT'. Unfortunately, the footprints turned out to be those of a hippo, and all from the same leg – presumably a stuffed one.

In 1934, a sceptical public was convinced again when a photograph by a surgeon named R.K. Wilson revealed the monster's slender neck and head rising out of the water. The surgeon's photograph has now became the most famous picture of the elusive creature.

It's a pity that this photograph, used by so many publications as absolute proof of Nessie, is not the same picture that R.K. Wilson took. The famous picture is cropped so that only the surrounding water is visible. The entire photograph, rarely ever seen, shows the shore of Loch Ness as well. With the shore visible, the size of the monster is in perspective and shows it to be about the size of a duck, which it also happens to strongly resemble. Other conveniently forgotten factors are the fact that the photograph was taken on April Fool's Day and that Wilson's own son admitted the photograph was fake.

The scientific community finally tried to inject some common sense into the matter. Dr F.A. Bather pointed out that the floor of Loch Ness was completely flat. A race of giant creatures living there for millions of years would have left so many skeletal remains that nobody could miss them if they were trying. Realising he was totally outclassed in the scientific department, Gould admitted that the Loch Ness Monster couldn't be a plesiosaur after all. Despite Gould's turnaround, and his theory having more holes than Swiss cheese, the plesiosaur explanation is still the most popular today.

The Nessie debacle continued. A businessman named Edward Mountain, mounted a full-scale expedition to prove the monster's existence and hired a team of unemployed locals to sit by the loch and watch for it. They saw the monster dozens of times and provided Mountain with a staggering 21 photographs in the first 2 weeks. It then occurred to Mountain that the men were employed only as long as the hunt was successful and were getting paid extra for sightings.

He had a few quiet words with his employees and the sightings stopped.

Once again, Nessie's fame began to wane and monster believers began to clutch at straws. In 1952, John Cobb crashed and died on Loch Ness trying to break the world water speed record. A wake from the monster was blamed even though Cobb's own team admitted the wake was from one of their boats.

But most people, looking back on the furore, began to question why previous sightings had varied so much in size and shape and Nessie became a bit of a joke.

In the nick of time came the publication of *More than a Legend: The Story of the Loch Ness Monster*. Written in 1957, by Constance Whyte, it offered an explanation for the discrepancies in the appearance of the monster over the years. There were, she proudly claimed, lots of monsters in Loch Ness.

Whyte's theory made Gould look like Einstein.

Astonishingly, the public accepted Constance Whyte's explanation, not realising the rest of the book was riddled with inaccuracies. (Whyte's 'explanation' for no sightings before 1932 was that there was no road by the loch until then – a statement that simply isn't true.)

Whyte's book was immensely popular and was immediately followed, with the usual uncanny timing, by a piece of film, a dramatic photograph and the first land sighting for 25 years. Loch Ness fever descended on the world again.

By the early '60s monster mania was in full swing and myth, hearsay and gossip had long since replaced the truth. Claims were now made by Nessie supporters of Loch Ness Monster sightings throughout history.

The creature, supposedly, appears on Neolithic carvings (they are actually Pictish serpent symbols, found all over Scotland). It was reported by the Roman historian, Dio Cassius (not true), vanquished by St Columba (only one of many fantastic stories about Columba's encounters with strange wildlife and taking place on the River Ness), reported by the historian Hector Boece (again, not Loch Ness) and sighted by eighteenth-century soldier, Patrick Rose (who in fact doesn't mention a monster but a floating mass of vegetation). It also turned up in the works of Daniel Defoe and nineteenth century issues of the *Glasgow Evening News* and the *Atlanta Constitution*. (all urban myths).

If there were going to be ancient sightings of a Loch Ness Monster, it would be reasonable to assume they'd come from people who actually lived on Loch Ness. Urquhart Castle, for instance, has occupied a prime site there and was inhabited from the Dark Ages until 1715. For the last two centuries, the loch has been regularly traversed by highlanders, lowland and English troops, sailing and fishing boats and tourists. Yet until 1932, nobody, it seems, ever spotted anything.

Coincidentally, the tourist trade, flourishing since Victorian times, had been drying up around the 1930s. This trade was briskly revived after each spate of monster sightings.

Considering the large number of sightings, there have been astonishingly few photographs of the monster. Millions of visitors pass Loch Ness each year, each hoping to photograph the creature on the way past. Yet the pictures which have been taken seem to show different creatures – and almost none show the shore or any object which would give some perspective. Many could be snaps of a garden pond just as easily as Loch Ness.

The exception is a famous picture taken by P.A. McNab in 1955. It shows a long black object with two humps near to what is, undeniably, Urquhart Castle. Using the castle for reference, the size of this monster can be accurately gauged. One of the humps *alone* measures around 55 feet. Unless there are two monsters, Nessie would have to be at least 70 feet long.

This was pretty good going for a creature that, 20 years earlier, measured less than 10 feet.

The last great monster photograph was taken in the 1970s, when an underwater camera caught what appeared to be a giant flipper passing in the loch. The flipper appears in only two frames – even though the camera shot 20,000 frames and caught no other part of any monster. This led some to speculate that the flippers were a hoax by local fishermen or even by the photographic team. The idea that a monster-hunting team might fake evidence was treated with horror by Nessie's supporters. That it had happened before was of no consequence, nor was the fact that one of the team leaders, Peter Rimes, offered to sell the photographs to *National Geographic*, then *Time* Magazine for $100 000.

Many aspects of the flipper photographs raise doubts. Why was a copy and not the original frame sent for enhancement? Why are the pictures so fuzzy when the camera took perfectly clear pictures of other marine life? Rhines presented the photographs to a team of experts, who concluded that the image could easily be the flipper of a fish blown up to appear much larger. They added, 'The photographs do not constitute acceptable evidence of the existence of a large living animal.'

Rhines then had the images computer enhanced but never released the results. This is an odd move to make – unless, of course, the enhancement showed the flipper to belong to a fish after all.

With millions of visitors snapping away, it is inevitable that every wind, water and boat wake, every rock, otter and floating log – in fact anything that ever ruffled the surface of Loch Ness – has been captured on film. It's also a sad fact that it is very easy to fake monster pictures – so much so that photographs aren't considered evidence anymore by most investigators.

It is far more difficult to fake a monster on film. Perhaps this is why, on a loch seething with visitors sporting video cameras, there has only ever been one vaguely credible moving picture of Nessie.

Convinced of the monster's existence by (disingenuous) books and articles, an unemployed worker named Tim Dinsdale made a two-day drive to Loch Ness in 1960, in order to capture the creature on film. With enviable optimism, Dinsdale gave himself only four days before having to return south. On day four, miraculously, he filmed Nessie. Encouraged, he stayed another day and managed to film it again! Both films are blurry and show an unidentified black object moving through in the water. If the object wasn't the wake of some small boat, the monster was now around 90 feet long.

The long distance and poor quality of the films make it impossible to tell what the object actually is, but Dinsdale was watching the object through X7 binoculars. The first object, he later admitted, was a mass of floating vegetation – but the second, he was sure, was a monster. It was Dinsdale's insistence that he could clearly see Nessie through the binoculars which leant the second film its credibility.

Unlike many Nessie hunters, Dinsdale seems to have genuine integrity. But during his entire trip, he hadn't slept more than three hours a night. He thought he had filmed the monster once, only to realise he was wrong – and had one last chance to film it again before slipping into obscurity. Dinsdale wanted to see the monster so much, it isn't hard to see why he did.

Yet one only has to go to the same spot and look through X7 binoculars to see that nobody could get a good look at an object in the loch unless it was the size of an aircraft carrier.

This does not stop monster enthusiasts from pointing to an official report, which they claim states that the object appears to be animate. The report in fact says that the object, *if it is not a speedboat*, appears to be animate.

Whatever Dinsdale thought he saw, it was enough to make him dedicate his life to hunting Nessie. Unlike so many monster hunters, he did not claim to have seen the monster dozens of times – and always when he had left his camera out of reach. Nor did he foist upon the public dubious photographs of fuzzy black floating lumps. Dinsdale hunted the monster for another quarter of a century but, hampered by his own honesty, he never produced an image of anything on Loch Ness again.

Monster hunters are now a permanent feature of Loch Ness and their resources grow with each decade. Early technology was prone to misinterpreting gas bubbles or shoals of fish as a hulking underwater creature – but every year, as the technology gets more sophisticated, it is less of an ally to the devoted. The loch caves where the monsters were thought to hide do not exist. The floor has been dredged and no remains or fossils were found. If there is a giant creature in the loch, improved technology should mean increased sightings. Instead, they have virtually disappeared.

It is, of course, impossible to prove that the Monster doesn't exist. But this is not Bigfoot in the vast forests of America or the Yeti on the unexplored ranges of the Himalayas. This is a creature the size of a double-decker bus trying to hide in a 23 mile long loch in the tourist centre of an industrialised country, obsessively hunted for 70 years and looked for by millions of visitors with cameras.

It's the eyewitness accounts that now keep the Loch Ness legend alive. Time and time again, families of motorists happily see what professional monster watchers with high-powered binoculars miss a few hundred yards down the road. Anyone who sights the creature refuses to believe they have been fooled by a trick of the light or water – even though a 1904 Royal Geographical Society Bathymetrical survey of Loch Ness (almost 20 years before the first sighting) actually added an appendix to its report called 'Mirages on Loch Ness'. In it, they stated: 'A kind of mirage is among the most familiar phenomena in Loch Ness . . . It is best seen in the morning'.

Monster hunters insist, not surprisingly, that morning is the best time to sight Nessie.

Enthusiasts don't list the vast number of monster sightings that turned out to be something else when the sightee actually had the opportunity to get closer. They refuse to accept that they have seen an otter, crested grebe, duck, speedboat, trawler, unusual wave formation, rock, string of geese flying low over the water, salmon leaping, or deer swimming.

Thanks to a thriving, monster-based tourist industry, visitors vastly outnumber locals at Loch Ness. Yet eyewitness reports by local people make up a larger percentage of monster sightings. Many more inhabitants insist the monster is real because a relative or a friend has seen it.

Anyone getting a clear film of Nessie would become very rich indeed. Yet none of the locals carry cameras or camcorders – despite their claim to know the monster exists.

Wouldn't you?

I THINK THEREFORE OCH AYE

Science is of no party. It seeks no object, selfish or unselfish, good or bad. It is unmoved by any emotion; it feels no pity, nor is it stirred by any wrong. Its sole aim is the investigation of truth and the discovery of law, wholly indifferent to the use to which these investigations and those discoveries may afterwards be put.

ARTHUR JAMES BALFOUR (1848–1930), BRITISH PRIME MINISTER

It is probably in the domain of science and technology that the Scots have consistently dazzled. A far larger nation would be justifiably proud of the scale of Scots creations and discoveries.

Scotland, of course, has produced its share of non-momentous inventions – the macintosh, the kaleidoscope, Bovril, the grand piano, the lawnmower, the speedometer, the print roller, compressed air, marmalade, cotton reels and thread, artificial lime juice, Christmas cards, the handkerchief . . . to name just a few.

What is extraordinary is the sheer impact that other Scottish innovations have had on mankind. Not once or twice, but time and time again, inventions attributed to the Scots have profoundly affected the world. Scots, or their immediate descendants, have been responsible for the steam boat, telegraph, radar, transistor, fax, pocket calculator, copier, calculus, logarithms, decimal point, insulin, chloroform, penicillin, cloning, telephone, television and the steam engine. (One could mention that Scots invented the double-acting, two-stroke, steeple, oscillating, heated - air and z-crank engines as well – but that might seem like boasting.)

The population of Scotland is only 5 million; and only about 23 million of the earth's 5.7 billion inhabitants are Scots by descent – less than 0.5 per cent. Yet almost 11 per cent of all Nobel Prizes have been awarded to Scots by birth or descent.

Scotsmen are considered to be the fathers of applied rheology, osmics, sociology, economics, rational philosophy, mineral optics, neurology, naval medicine, crystallography, pharmacology, weather forecasting, chemotherapeutics, experimental geology, gynaecology, geology, experimental optics, antiseptic surgery, electronics, oceanography, military medicine, naval architecture, obstetrics and mathematical morphology. One can see why Scots schoolchildren aren't asked to memorise the list.

The following run-through of Scottish innovations shows even more clearly just what a difference Scots innovators have made to the world.

AGRICULTURE: It isn't surprising that Scots had a hand in important agricultural innovations – large parts of Scotland have the kind of landscape that needs to be battled rather than farmed. The mass exodus of Scots to America, and some of the finest farming land in the world, prompted another explosion of agricultural ingenuity. The reason these achievements did not gain huge recognition? Well. When was the last time *you* had a conversation about advances in farming methods?

Michael Menzies developed the threshing machine around 1743, which was then vastly improved by another Scot named Andrew Meikle; and in 1786, James Small of Scotland invented the revolutionary swing plough. (The subsoil plough was also invented in Scotland.) In 1827 Patrick Bell of Carmyllie invented the reaper, though he didn't develop the idea and faded into obscurity; while David Fife, a Canadian Scot, developed the first hard spring wheat in North America. The milking machine was then invented by William Murchland in Scotland in 1891.

MEDICINE: John Hunter (1728–93) pioneered the art of tissue grafting and the science of pathology and was the father of modern surgery – turning it from the part-time trade of barbers into a respectable science.

Unfortunately, he died of a heart attack brought on by a fit of rage. His brother, a much calmer chap, founded the science of gynaecology. Scotsman Alexander Skene (1837–1900) went on to establish gynaecology in the US and found the American Gynaecological Society, while a Scotswoman named Marie Carmichael Stopes (1880–1958) pioneered birth control – opening Britain's first birth control clinic in 1921.

Although Englishman William Jenner is credited with discovering the vaccination against smallpox in 1796, it appears that a Scottish physician named Charles Maitland vaccinated 85 people in London against the disease between 1721 and 1723. John Leslie (1766–1832) discovered blood capillary action and invented the differential thermometer, the hygrometer and the photometer. Meanwhile James Syme (1799–1870) caused an astonishing upturn in the confidence and expertise of new doctors by being the first surgeon to have students present at consultations – a sight now familiar on TV medical dramas all over the world.

James Young Simpson (1811–70) entered Edinburgh University at 14, a sign that he might be destined for great things. Sure enough, he went on to invent chloroform, alleviating the pain of the millions who would undergo surgery in the future. He was also the first person to use anaesthesia in childbirth. The importance of this process is heartily endorsed by mothers worldwide today, despite his discovery being frowned on at the time by those who thought the pain of childbirth was part of the curse of Eve.

Bizarrely enough, the acceptance of chloroform stopped dead the work of another Scot working in India, James Esdaile (1808–59), who was the first man to perform operations under a completely different form of anaesthetic – which he called hypnotism.

Joseph Lister (1827–1912), London-trained, but at one time a house surgeon at Edinburgh Royal Infirmary, was the first man to insist that surgery should only be carried out under antiseptic conditions. What seems obvious to us now, and has saved millions of lives, was fiercely resisted by older doctors whose ancient blood-encrusted frock coats were treasured status symbols. Lister also invented catgut stitching and gauze dressing for wounds. He is not to be confused with Scotsman Robert Liston (1794–1847), who performed the first operation under general anaesthesia, invented the bone-cutting forceps and the Liston splint, and performed the first successful removal of a shoulder blade.

Sir Patrick Manson (1844–1922) theorised that parasitic diseases were caused by biting insects; and these theories were confirmed by Sir Ronald Ross, son of a Scottish general, and a Nobel Prize winner, who discovered the cycle of the malaria parasite and how the disease was spread. Between them they were probably responsible for saving more human lives than virtually anyone in world history.

Sir William McEwan (1848–1924) evolved many techniques of brain surgery, introduced the mastoid operation, the first bone graft, the lung operation, the first training course for nurses and, most impressively, the first operation to fix knock-knees.

John McIntyre (1857–1928) pioneered X-ray techniques and founded the world's first radiological department. John McLeod (1876–1935) won the Nobel Prize for discovering insulin in 1923.

Alexander Fleming (1881–1995) discovered penicillin – which, for years, made no impression whatsoever on the scientific community. Then the Second World War came along. Fleming received a knighthood in 1994 and shared the Nobel Prize for medicine.

In recent years Ian Donald (1910–) invented the hospital ultrasonic scanner, and the pregnancy scanner; and in 1988 Sir James Black won the Nobel Prize for inventing Beta-Blockers and Tagamet.

INDUSTRY: James Watt (1736–1819) invented the steam engine, a concept that provided the impetus for the Industrial Revolution and altered the western world forever. After his invention, factories could be built anywhere and powered travel on land and sea was an inevitability. His birthday is not celebrated by nature lovers.

Watt also came up with steam heat, the revolution counter and the centrifugal governor – the beginning of automated machines. He provided the definition of 'horsepower' and got its unit of power, the 'watt', named after him as a reward. He developed the principle of the gasometer, popularised the slide rule and – oddly enough – was the first person to reverse a ship's engine. He invented the first letter copier and had the idea for the screw propeller over half a century before it was used.

When the screw propeller finally did make a physical appearance in 1827, it was Scotsman Robert Wilson, who invented it.

William Murdoch (1754–1839) showed his practical side early on by sculpting an expensive-looking hat out of wood for use in interviews. More importantly, he was the inventor of gaslight. He also built the first experimental model of a locomotive, in 1785, but did not patent it. His model was spotted by Englishman Richard Trevithick, who did patent it (17 years later). The eventual inventor of the practical locomotive was George Stephenson – whose parents were Scottish.

John Louden McAdam (1756–1836) developed the principles of road making that are still used to this day – making the word 'Tarmac' (short for Tar-McAdam) part of everyday language. Thomas Telford (1757–1834) was arguably the greatest civil engineer of all time and trained a generation of builders. Scotland turned into the world leader in civil engineering: Edinburgh University taught the subject quarter of a century before the rest of Europe. Telford also introduced the concept of using building contractors – a fundamental, but very annoying, part of today's society.

James Chalmers (1782–1853) produced the world's first stick-on postage stamp. Credit for this innovation, used in every country in the world, is usually given to Englishman Rowland Hill. However, Hill put forward the idea in print in 1837 and Chalmers had already printed his first stamp in Dundee three years earlier. Chalmers then, helpfully, invented the postmark.

Scotland can also lay claim to having the first mail-van service and the first post office, while Scot Andrew Hamilton, organised the first postal service in North America. Scots engineer Sandford Fleming designed the first Canadian stamp and was instrumental in setting up the world time zones. Scotland also produced the postcard and the picture postcard – ensuring there would be even more things to post.

James Neilson (1792–1865) invented the hot blast furnace, which revolutionized the iron industry, as well as creating the fishtail gas burner; while James Naysmith (1808–90) invented the steam hammer, the pile driver and – naturally enough, when you think of how it feels – the dentist's drill. He also created standardised automatic machine tools, making mass production of objects possible for the first time.

Robert Mushet (1811–91) discovered cast steel, though the credit for it was stolen by an industrialist named Bessemer (whose application of the same process was fundamentally flawed). Mushet also invented self-hardening tool steel.

James Young (1811–83) was known as 'Paraffin Young'. Not surprisingly, he invented paraffin. He also devised the process of petroleum oil refining, created the world's first oil refinery and was pivotal in building up the American oil industry. Then, just in case the world's oil suddenly ran out, he invented the process for extracting oil from shale.

Kirkpatrick MacMillan (1813–78) lays claim to the invention of the first bicycle and, ironically, was fined for committing the first cycling offence when he ran over a small child. His unwieldy invention prompted fellow Scot, John Dunlop (1840–1921), to develop the pneumatic tyre for his bike wheels. Dunlop went on to become rich and Dunlop tyres are still famous the world over. To his astonishment, Dunlop then discovered that he had not actually invented the pneumatic tyre. It had been patented some years before by yet another Scot, R.W. Thomson (1822–73).

Dunlop redeemed himself by patenting the first self-acting fountain pen, the first portable steam crane and the first tractor.

Then there was Frederick Creed (1871–1957), born of Scottish parents in Nova Scotia, who arrived in Scotland and revolutionised the communications industry by inventing the teleprinter.

SCIENCE: The mathematician John Napier (1550–1617) devised the principle of fractional indices, logarithms and the decimal point – to the delight of schoolchildren all over the world. He freed scientists forever from the mundane calculations that massively slowed their work. The impact of these discoveries, in his day, was similar to the invention of the computer in the twentieth century. In fact, 'Napier's Bones' – a series of numbered rods used to facilitate multiplication and division – amounted to the world's first computing device. (Centuries later, in 1916, Scotsman James Graham Johnstone, along with a Scottish American named Thomas Watson, developed a tabulating machine – basically a prototype computer – to help their debt-ridden company Computing-Tabulating-Recording. It worked. The company became IBM – until recently the most profitable enterprise in existence.)

John Napier also found time to become a religious author and design several particularly nasty weapons for use against the Spanish.

James Gregory (1638–75) invented the reflecting telescope, the first clock to record split-seconds and the achromatic lens. He was actually related to the notorious MacGregors (of Rob Roy fame), but his family was forced to change their surname when it became outlawed. Gregory also set up hours of fun for subsequent generations of schoolchildren by developing the principles of calculus, while Scot Duncan Gregory founded modern algebra.

James Hutton (1726–97) is known as the 'Father of Modern Geology'. He correctly theorized how the earth was formed, then went on to provide proof of its rotation. His work was popularised by another Scot, John Playfair, and Sir James Hall completed the trio as 'Father of Experimental Geology'. Hutton's theories were expanded by Scotsman, Sir Charles Lyell, who convinced Darwin to pursue his evolutionary ideas. Coincidentally enough, Hutton is buried directly opposite Lord Monboddo's unmarked grave in Greyfriars Churchyard in Edinburgh.

Continental drift and plate tectonics were first described by Thomas

Dick from Angus. He came up with the widely ridiculed theory that the continents had once been joined – now accepted as true. Scots went on to invent the seismometer, found the science of seismology, present the idea that the earth's orbit affects long-term climate changes, and conduct what was probably the world's first geological survey.

Joseph Black (1728–99) identified carbon monoxide long before it hung in easily observed clouds over several major cities. He also came up with the Theory of Combustion, discovered specific heat and introduced the manufacture of writing-paper. Robert Brown (1773–1858) discovered, naturally enough, Brownian Motion – the first observed evidence of atomism. He also discovered the nucleus of the cell, the starting point for all life.

George MacKenzie (1780–1848) realized that carbon and diamonds were chemically identical, thus saving young men a lifetime of hard toil paying for one ring, while Thomas Graham (1805–69) formulated the principle of the diffusion of gases, the principle of the separation of gases, and the principles of dialysis.

Alexander Bain (1810–77) invented the electric clock and the electromagnetic pendulum – which led to the adoption of Greenwich Mean Time. He may well have invented the telegraph, but sold his model for £3 to Charles Wheatstone who is now credited with the invention. He did, however, patent an automatic recording telegraph and was arguably the first person to send a facsimile.

William Thomson, Lord Kelvin (1824–1907) entered Glasgow University at the age of ten – the youngest undergraduate in history. As an adult he calculated absolute zero temperature and devised the temperature scale named after him. He predated Einstein with a version of the second law of thermodynamics and coined the term 'kinetic energy' as well as developing the wave theory of light and the field of molecular dynamics. He designed a device to measure the absolute measurement of currents, invented the mirror galvanometer, the electric strain gauge, the siphon recorder, the ampere balance and the electrostatic voltmeter. He also found time to become a champion rower and founded the Glasgow University Musical Society.

The achievements of James Clerk Maxwell (1831–79) have only recently been fully appreciated by the scientific community, where he is now regarded on a par with Newton and Einstein. Einstein himself acknowledged his debt to Maxwell's work, calling it 'the most fruitful that physics has experienced since the time of Newton', and even kept a picture of Maxwell on his wall. Physicist Richard Feynman said of Maxwell: there can be little doubt that the most significant event of the nineteenth century will be judged as Maxwell's discovery of the laws of electrodynamics.'

Maxwell developed the kinetic theory of gases, founded the science of statistical mechanics and originated the concept of cybernetics. It would be fair to say that he altered the whole course of scientific thinking, turning the tide from classical to modern physics. He then came up with the theory of electromagnetism – fundamental to the future science of electronics and putting Einstein, in his own words, 'on the road' to his discoveries. Not satisfied with that, Maxwell went on to produce the theory of colour blindness. Then, just to rub it in, he made the first colour photograph.

Henry Faulds (1843–1930) came up with the idea of fingerprinting criminals while working in Tokyo. Unfortunately, he had a hard time convincing the police forces of the world of the benefits of this innovation and, to begin with, only the police of Buenos Aires bothered to use it. The Scots went on to corner the baddie-detecting market when Scotsman Sir Andrew Noble perfected the science of ballistics.

Sir James Dewar (1847–1932) pioneered cryogenic research, provided the scientist Kekule with the formula for benzine and invented the thermos flask.

As the inventor of the telephone, Alexander Graham Bell (1847–1922) has assured his place in history. Interestingly, he also whipped up a metal detector to locate a bullet inside the body of US President Garfield, who was dying after an assassination attempt. It might even have worked if Garfield hadn't been lying on a bedful of steel springs. Following on from Bell's lead, the world's first telephone exchange was established in 1879, in Glasgow.

Sir William Ramsay (1852–1916) won the Nobel Prize for discovering the inert family of gases. He also made his own scientific glassware, since he counted glassblowing among his many talents. In 1927 Charles Wilson (1869–1959) also won the Nobel Prize for the invention of the cloud chamber – described by the scientist Rutherford as 'The most original piece of apparatus in the whole history of Science' – which could make a trail of electrically charged particles visible. Suddenly scientists, after years of painstaking guesswork could actually see how atoms and atomic physics worked.

Then, looking at the big picture, rather than the subatomic one, Wilson became the first man to investigate cosmic radiation. In matters extra-terrestrial, Scots also put forward the nebular theory of astronomy, the measurement of the distance of a fixed star and the explanation of sunspots.

John Logie Baird (1888–1946) came up with one of the most influential inventions in human history – the television. There has been debate over whether or not Baird really deserves this accolade, since his version of television was not the one that eventually went into production. (Baird's television had a mechanical scanner and was not the high resolution television of today.) Be that as it may, there is no doubt that the first television transmission of a moving picture of any sort was made by Baird, on 30 October 1925.

Baird then went on to produce the first colour television transmission and developed a system called 'Phonovision', which allowed owners to record images on to aluminium disc. In effect, he had invented the first video player. But when the more effective electrical system went into production, Baird's mechanically based television was dropped and the discs became useless.

The modern version of television, however, owes its existence to Scotsman Alan Swinton (1863–1930), who formulated its principles and invented its essential component – the cathode ray tube.

Tireless in his endeavours, Logie Baird also developed Noctovision (allowing sight in the dark) and 3D television. Hampered by ill health and poverty for much of his life, Baird kept himself financially afloat by producing Osmo Boot Polish, Speedy Cleaner Soap and Baird's Trinidad Jam. He even tried to turn coal dust into diamonds while working at a power plant – he managed to black out the city of Glasgow for 11 minutes and was fired.

Sir Robert Watson Watt (1892–1973) was inventor of a system that opened up the world by allowing the flow of air traffic across the globe – radio detection and ranging – more commonly known as radar. Sir Alexander Robertus Todd (1907–) won the Nobel Prize for chemistry in 1957, setting the stage for the discovery of DNA.

The number of world-class Scottish innovations, sadly, began to decline rapidly after the industrial revolution. The flow of Scots from their home country weakened Scotland's scientific influence immeasurably. Innovations to which Scotland might have laid claim were now being made in other countries, by descendents of Scots who had emigrated; and the slowly eroding standards of education in Scotland didn't help either.

But, just when it looked like Scotland's inventing machine had ground to a halt, Dr Ian Wilmut made the first clone – Dolly the Sheep – in 1997, at the Roslin Institute, just outside Edinburgh. In June 2000, his team followed this up with the world's first genetically modified clones.

Whether this is a good thing, or not, has been widely debated. Robert Louis Stevenson and Mary Shelley would have had a field day with the prospect. Yet these Scottish innovations may well prove to be the most significant scientific discoveries in the history of mankind.

The Scots are not done yet.

THE TWO SECRET HISTORIES
OF SCOTLAND

When truth becomes legend – print the legend.
JAMES WARNER BELLAH, *THE MAN WHO SHOT LIBERTY VALANCE*

So, what are the two secret histories of Scotland? In a sense, they are not histories at all. Rather, they are two sides of a nation that have been buried or forgotten.

It is easy to see why anything fake or unsavoury in Caledonian history would be played down. If you have skeletons in your cupboard, you pretty much want them to stay there. In that respect, all nations have a hidden nasty past – this book just happens to be about Scotland's.

But why is there another secret history? Scotland is rightfully proud of its inventiveness and influence, but a huge number of spectacular innovators have been forgotten. This book has listed only a few of them.

It seems we are so proud of our own myth that we don't feel the need to search for unsung heroes. As with our national anthem, it is enough for many Scots to be proud of the sentiment and recognise the tune – who cares if they don't know all the verses?

The Emperor's New Kilt is not an extensive history of the Scottish nation – it has simply dipped into the country's past to illustrate its hidden treasures and secret curses. The hidden treasure is a wealth of innovation that is barely known. The secret curse is that the Scots are a nation bred for everyday violence. And that violence has been mythologised into a brave thing. A noble thing.

A good thing.

Robert Louis Stevenson captured the two secret histories of Scotland perfectly. Dr Jekyll is the good guy, the admirable but boring inventor. Hyde is the bad guy, self-obsessed and ultra-violent, but gloriously full of beans.

In the end, the aim of *The Emperor's New Kilt* is not just to uncover historical truths. Truth, like history, is subjective. It does not matter, in the end, whether King Arthur was Scottish or Welsh. What matters is that he was not a magical knight in shining armour but a primitive, savage warlord. That is the lesson to be learnt in looking at what any country has hidden. We have to accept the dark side of Scottish history, the ever-present Mr Hyde. Like Dr Jekyll, we can't simply banish him by refusing to admit he exists or that he isn't part of our national consciousness.

Scotland has a duality more apparent than in any other country. It permeates every strata of its national existence. The Highlands and the Lowlands. The Protestant and the Catholic. The generosity and the meanness. The aggressor and the underdog. Glasgow and Edinburgh. No other nation displays dualities of such breadth, depth and infinite variety.

We are the Jekyll-and-Hyde nation. What we have to accept is that Jekyll has a place in a civilised future.

Hyde does not.

There are Scots who have bought into the myth of their own country – that we were a generous, honourable, noble warrior race – though anyone who thinks war is noble has never seen a horse cut in half with a broadsword. Not everyone can be an inventor, but everyone can be noble or brave. These people are proud to be Scots because they think the Scots are like that.

There are other Scots who are simply proud to be Scots – it allows them to blame their excesses on something other than themselves. They mistake xenophobia for patriotism and they substitute bravery for savagery. Not everyone can be an inventor, but everyone can fight or hate.

This kind of mentality still exists among many Scots today. And there's no point in pretending that, after 1,000 years of war and hardship, it suddenly appeared out of nowhere.

Mr Hyde has always been with us.

Dr Jekyll had to kill himself to get rid of Mr Hyde. We do not. We have the magic potion that will keep him buried. Scotland has built up a myth of being a wonderful land, one that has always been peopled with generous noble, honourable warriors. So what if it isn't true? We should live up to it anyway.

The last verse of the Scottish national anthem declares proudly:

> Those days are past now and in the past they must remain
> But we can still rise now and be the nation again
> That stood against him . . .

It refers to a fight for independence that took place against the English, *seven hundred* years ago. Yet many Scots still regard the English with dislike, not because of any bad qualities they have, but because they are an enemy we never quite managed to beat – something on which we can blame our own flaws and failures on. The English, on the other hand, don't hate the Scots. They are indifferent to them. As far as England is concerned, if Scotland wants to see itself as a downtrodden victim, it can go right ahead.

Yet we once beat the English spectacularly. In the eighteenth and early nineteenth centuries, regardless of the fact that Scotland was newly united with its 'Auld Enemy', the Scottish Enlightenment blossomed – the south had nothing to match it. During that period Scottish intellectual achievement flourished to the extent that a tiny country was the world leader in science, technology and philosophy.

For a short time Dr Jekyll was stronger than Mr Hyde.

Perhaps it will happen again. Despite the fears of a whole world, Scotland has produced the first clone and the first genetically modified clone. If we do not have the strength of will to change our warrior nature, our own scientific innovators may do it for us.

There are two secret histories of Scotland. One is hidden because we'd rather pretend a savage past was an 'adventurous' one. The other is hidden because it reveals that our own ancestors have shown us up.

Everyone can fight, but not everyone can be an inventor.

Or can they?

The Scots national identity *is* the product of invention, in more ways than one. It is a bold, colourful creation that perfectly complements the real achievements of the Scottish Enlightenment. It befits a race that led the world in innovative thought.

Everyone can fight to keep that present.

SELECT BIBLIOGRAPHY

Aitchison, N., *MacBeth: Man and Myth* (Gloucestershire, 1999)

Ashe, G., *Land to the West* (London, 1962)

Black, G.F., *Scotland's Mark on America* (New York, 1921)

Boece, H., *Historia de Scotia* (Paris, 1527)

Boswell, J., *Journey to the Western Islands of Scotland* (Oxford, 1924)

Brander, M., *The Making of the Highlands* (London, 1980)

               The Emigrant Scots (London, 1982)

Bruce, D., *The Mark of the Scots* (New Jersey, 1996)

Buchanan, G., *The History of Scotland* (1690)

Burnet, J., *Of the Origin and Progress of Language* (1792)

Burton, J.H., *The Scot Abroad* (London, 1864)

Calder, J., *The Enterprising Scot* (Edinburgh, 1986)

Campbell, R.H., *Scotland Since 1707* (Oxford, 1977)

Cloyd, E.L., *James Burnett; Lord Monboddo* (Oxford, 1972)

Daiches, D., *The Paradox of Scottish Culture* (Oxford, 1964)

Dinsdale, T., *The Loch Ness Monster* (London, 1960)

Donaldson, G., *Scottish Kings* (London, 1967)

Ellis, H., *A Study of British Genius* (Boston, 1926)

Famighetti, R. (ed.), *World Almanac and Book of Facts* (New York, 1999)

Gibbon, J.M., *Scots in Canada* (Toronto, 1911)

Goring, R. (ed.), *Chambers Scottish Biographical Dictionary* (Edinburgh, 1992)

Gray, M., *The Highland Economy* (London, 1957)

Haugard, E. (trans.), *Hans Andersen: His Classic Tales* (London, 1984)

Holinshed, R., *Chronicles of England, Scotland and Ireland* (London, 1577)

Hook, A., *Scotland and America* (Glasgow, 1957)

Hyde, H.M., *John Law* (London, 1969)

Kenyon, J.P., *The Stuarts: A Study in Kingship* (London, 1970)

McCosh, J., *The Scottish Philosophy* (New York, 1875)

MacKenzie, A., *A History of the Highland Clearances* (Glasgow, 1883)

Mackie, J.D., *A History of Scotland* (New York, 1964)

Manlove, C., *Scottish Fantasy Literature* (Edinburgh, 1994)

Morrison, L., *The History of the Sinclair Family in Europe and America for Eleven Hundred Years* (1896)

Munro, R.W., *Clansmen and Kinsmen* (Edinburgh, 1971)

Petras, K. and R. (ed.), *Very Bad Poetry* (London, 1997)

Pohl, F.J., *The Lost Discovery* (New York, 1952)

Prince Henry Sinclair (London, 1974)

Reed, A.H., *The Story of Early Dunedin* (Wellington, 1956)

Rich, E.E., *The History of the Hudson Bay Company* (London, 1958)

Ross, S., *Monarchs of Scotland* (Moffat, 1990)

Scotland's Cultural Heritage Unit, *Scots in Russia* (Edinburgh, 1987)

Shepperson, G., *The American Revolution and Scotland* (Norfolk, 1977)

Simpson, W.D., *Portrait of the Highlands* (London, 1969)

Steel, T., *Scotland's Story* (London, 1984)

Stewart, B., *MacBeth* (Dorset, 1988)

Stuart, A.F., *The Scots in Poland* (Edinburgh, 1913)

Watson, L., *Dark Nature* (London, 1995)

Whitelock, D. (ed.), *Anglo-Saxon Chronicle* (London, 1961)

Whyte, C., *More than a Legend?* (London, 1957)

Wills, E., *Scottish Firsts* (Glasgow, 1985)

Wyntoun, A.D.L. (ed.), *The Orygynale Cronykil of Scotland* (Edinburgh, 1879)